TO HELL AND BACK

In *To Hell and Back*, Steve Heird is refreshingly honest about his struggles with addiction as a well-respected physician. His humble nature, sense of humor, and raw honesty are inspiring, and his insights on healing and awareness will help many who are struggling in their darkest days to hold out for the hope and light available to us all.

—**Dina Proctor**, best-selling author of *Madly Chasing Peace: How I Went from Hell to Happy in Nine Minutes a Day*

When you lose your way on the journey of life, his mottoes to live by will guide you through the difficult times and help you to find your way. Dr. Steven Heird's experience can be your life coach and the guide you require so your pain becomes the labor pain of your self-birth.

—**Bernie Siegel**, M.D., author of *A Book of Miracles and The Art of Healing*

In your hands is a prescription unlike any you have ever had before. Once you read this book you will have something "refillable" that will never run out for a life you absolutely love living. This book is medicine for your Soul.

—**Mary Morrissey**, best-selling author of *No Less Than Greatness* and *Building Your Field of Dreams*

I have had the honor of working with Dr. Heird in various capacities. Finding his way from addiction to recovery, this surgeon has turned his powerful and effective method of healing and transformation into a series of prescriptions that will guide others to the truth about their addictions. *To Hell and Back* will light the path to extinguish the fear and self-doubt that come with the power of addiction and will lead one to self-love, self-trust, and freedom from limitation.

—**Esperanza Universal**, attorney, spiritual teacher, S.O.U.L. Institute Inc. [www.soulinstitute.com]

If you're looking for a light to guide your path from addiction to recovery, *To Hell and Back* will shine a healing truth to help you find your way. This surgeon's story of addiction is sure to teach you the power of perseverance and the importance of awareness.

—**Michael Harris**, best-selling author and business coach

Receive a prescription like no other with this candid and enlivening story of one surgeon's path from addiction to recovery. Take time to nurture your soul with this honest account of the importance of awareness when it matters most.

—**Gay Hendricks**, Ph.D., author of *The Big Leap* and *Conscious Loving*

Wow what a journey Steven. A journey that took me into a mental movie seeing every part of your story as you expressed it so vividly, the story came alive for me. Powerful, personal, authentic and gutsy—real narration that we can all relate to as humans, as healthcare professionals, and as people seeking fulfillment from the outside-in. Thank you for your courage in sharing your life learnings so openly with the world. I agree 100% with your Twelve Prescriptions.

What kept jolting me out of the movie scenes while reading the book were the revelations neatly built into the text, that made me STOP and ponder, deeply. I quote some of those Moments of Truth from your book:

"I was convinced that getting ahead would make me happy. When I get there, then it's going to all feel perfect. For some reason, I was never satisfied."

"That tiny obstacle to learning the truth gave me a good excuse to remain in denial."

"Being an addict doesn't suppress the goodness within you. It temporarily sequesters what you fear so you don't have to deal with it."

"This small thought of gratitude seemed to create the smallest crack of light in my consciousness. My mind's eye began to experience a stream of images."

"My tears flowed. I'm okay just the way I am? I don't need to do anything to be loved? I'm loved! I know it and feel it! I am LOVED! I AM love! I became one with that love at that moment."

Dr. Heird's book is a must read for everyone seeking personal growth, self-redemption, and connection with others and the Divine Power. While underpinning that we are mere mortal humans, living only to express our souls' higher purpose on this Earth—which is to eventually reconnect with The One, The Origin, The Destiny of Love.

—**Dr. Hisham Abdalla**, best-selling author of
4D Leadership: Master the 4D's of Success and Live your Dreams

TO HELL AND BACK

A SURGEON'S STORY OF ADDICTION

12 Prescriptions for Awareness

STEVEN B. HEIRD, MD, FACS

NEW YORK

TO HELL AND BACK
A SURGEON'S STORY OF ADDICTION
12 Prescriptions for Awareness

Published in New York, New York, by Morgan James Publishing. Morgan James and The Entrepreneurial Publisher are trademarks of Morgan James, LLC. www.MorganJamesPublishing.com

The Morgan James Speakers Group can bring authors to your live event. For more information or to book an event visit The Morgan James Speakers Group at www.TheMorganJamesSpeakersGroup.com.

A FREE eBook edition is available
with the purchase of this print book

CLEARLY PRINT YOUR NAME IN THE BOX ABOVE

Instructions to claim your free eBook edition:
1. Download the BitLit app for Android or iOS
2. Write your name in UPPER CASE in the box
3. Use the BitLit app to submit a photo
4. Download your eBook to any device

ISBN 978-1-63047-234-4 paperback
ISBN 978-1-63047-235-1 eBook
ISBN 978-1-63047-236-8 hardcover
Library of Congress Control Number:
2014937579

Cover Design by:
Rachel Lopez
www.r2cdesign.com

Interior Design by:
Bonnie Bushman
bonnie@caboodlegraphics.com

In an effort to support local communities, raise awareness and funds, Morgan James Publishing donates a percentage of all book sales for the life of each book to Habitat for Humanity Peninsula and Greater Williamsburg.

Get involved today, visit
www.MorganJamesBuilds.com

Habitat
for Humanity®
Peninsula and
Greater Williamsburg
Building Partner

Dedication

I dedicate this book to my loving mother and father for their unwavering faith and support for me throughout this entire journey. Thank you, mom, for reading my favorite childhood book *The Little Engine That Could* to me over and over—the story still inspires me to this day.

Contents

Foreword

When Steve Heird asked me to write the Foreword for his book I felt instantly grateful ... grateful to be a part of something (this book) that has the potential to positively impact many people in the world.

The book you are holding in your hands reads like a gripping novel that you will not want to put down. I met Steve and discovered his amazing story when he attended a program that I was co-delivering. What struck me most about Steve wasn't just his story, but his exceptional energy and his gift to inspire those who came into contact with him. He is the essence of love and authenticity. Many people will be able to relate to parts of Steve's experience, but what is more important are the valuable lessons he has grasped as a result of going through something that literally kills many people.

As a medical doctor Steve prescribes medications for his patients. In *To Hell and Back* Steve is offering a different type of prescription—prescriptions that don't have unpleasant side effects. Sure, they have side effects, but only the most amazingly wonderful kind.

As much as Steve's journey is a spellbinding story, he wraps up this great piece of work with the most incredible, life-changing prescriptions for awareness that I've had the pleasure of being exposed to. They say "save the best till last" and that's what you'll find in this book.

After you read the chapters containing Steve's story, my suggestion is to follow Steve's advice. He's wise. He not only has the knowledge of what it takes to have a healthy, enlightened, and fulfilling way of life, he lives it and he can help you do the same. In the back of this book you will find the prescriptions for awareness. After you finish reading the entire book, go back and print them and have them become a part of your day. I'm certain that when you do, you will live a more bountiful, enjoyable, and gratifying life.

—**Peggy McColl**, New York Times Best-Selling Author

Acknowledgments

I would like to express my sincere gratitude to the many people who have provided wonderful support in my life and, especially, in the creation of this book. Let me begin where I first experienced healing at Marworth Rehabilitation Center. I thank Michelle K., my counselor, and Dominick, program director, of the Marworth staff.

I also acknowledge the Weekend Steps AA Home Group for assisting in my continued recovery. And, a special thanks to my first sponsor, Ken S., who was instrumental in guiding me through the early days of the consequences of my disease.

I gratefully acknowledge all of the participants of the SuperMind program for their support and encouragement, and a special thank you to the four mentors: Peggy McColl, Gay Hendricks, Bob Proctor, and Mary Morrissey.

A special thank you to Peggy McColl who welcomed me into her home and stuck with me, giving me the encouragement to begin this book. I thank Nancy Peske for putting my thoughts and experiences into words, and I express my sincere gratitude to all who reviewed this manuscript and provided testimonials in support of my efforts.

I thank Candy Scott, for her creative advice and for introducing me to the awesome healing power of Bikram yoga, and Sandra Galvagny, for her creative and spiritual guidance. I also thank Dr. Steve Pandelidis, my professional colleague and friend, for his continued support through bad times and good. I would like to acknowledge the late Gary Hopson Dobbs III, the college professor instrumental in teaching me to study hard, and to Dr. James S. Starling, for his inspiration to keep the pursuit of my dreams alive.

Thank you to the following for their support of this book and my mission: Ken Silberstein, Deb Lyden, Vicky Giuffrida, Christina Wilson, Denyse Kling, Jacki Shaffer, Theia Light Center staff.

A special thanks to my only sibling Jesse who always answered my phone calls for help and advice.

A final thank you to those most important to my life, my wonderful sons and only daughter: Billy, Jonathan, Andrew, and Grace.

Introduction

I was the head of the Department of Vascular Surgery at a large community hospital, training surgical residents and performing very challenging, lifesaving surgeries—and I was proud of my accomplishments. I had met all my goals and forged my dreams into reality. I was a farm boy who used to help my dad with raising and slaughtering turkeys. My parents had graduated from high school with modest grades, but I grew up determined to become a skilled physician. And I have to say, I liked the money too.

Now, my parents would have been satisfied if I had simply graduated from college and settled into a decent job, however I aspired to be something more. I had to be creative in finding a path to my goal of becoming a surgeon, a goal I'd figured out when I was very young. I wasn't exactly a star student right away. It was hard for me to study and I didn't do well on tests, but I was able through trial and error—and perseverance—to meet those challenges. And on a personal front, I was able to have the family I had always wanted. I had an accomplished wife, three wonderful sons, and a beautiful little girl who we had recently adopted from China. We led a busy, middle class life in a lovely five-bedroom house in the suburbs of York, Pennsylvania. I was able to send my boys to good schools and was proud of my BMW. It was all paid for by my rapidly increasing financial worth—the result of long hours spent building a vascular surgery practice with my partners.

So, at age forty-nine, after having spent decades pursuing the American dream of a successful and happy life, I could confidently say that I had arrived. But looking back on the years leading up to the day my life did a 180, every time I reached a goal, I didn't stop to appreciate it. I always looked ahead, thinking, "When I get there, it will all be perfect." For some reason, I was never satisfied—I was always on the move. Every time I felt contented with a sense of completion or accomplishment, it slipped away almost instantly, and it wouldn't be long before I was off on another quest.

Maybe my problem was that I was an adrenaline junkie. I think I was born that way. I was always striving to get over the next hurdle or around the next obstacle. On one hand, the drive to challenge myself allowed me to achieve the successes I took pride in. It was a fast-paced life and included a lot of fun at times. I developed a passion for skiing, particularly helicopter skiing, where you're dropped from a helicopter onto a bowl of snow at the top of the mountain and make a pristine trail in the white powder as you fly down the slope. It was exhilarating! Raising my kids, running them to sporting events and cheering them on as they competed, gave me a rush as well. But no matter what I did to push myself, it wasn't long before a sense of emptiness rose within me and I'd look for the next goal to strive for. That part wasn't working for me. I couldn't help wondering, "If I don't have a goal, what's my purpose?" I was convinced that "getting ahead," as if I were in some sort of marathon toward a finish line, would make me happy. Yet whatever relief I felt on reaching my aim and experiencing a little joy slipped away quickly.

The empty feeling inside me was so uncomfortable that I tried to fill it with addictive behaviors, whether it was exercise, work, sex, thinking, or worrying. There was always something to be done. When there was a goal in front of me, I was dogged about reaching it—and often, very creative. But no matter what I did, I couldn't fill that hole. I always felt I hadn't accomplished enough—or more accurately, I wasn't enough. Now I know what I was really feeling and thinking all those years. It took a lot of hard work to recognize this truth about myself and why I couldn't stop running and simply be present with myself. I had to discover who I was and experience that I'm always loved. I don't have to earn anyone's approval to be worthy of love.

Here's what else I learned: Addiction is insidious. It snuck up on me despite the pleasure I felt when I was with my kids, or finishing up a successful surgery, or completing an afternoon run that I had almost skipped because I was exhausted from lack of sleep. I thought I was only using alcohol to unwind. I told myself that everyone drinks a few beers after work. The prescription drugs prevented hangovers and gave me more energy for a few hours, and didn't seem to have any side effects. I was in control, wasn't I? It sure looked that way from where I stood. But that's the stinking thinking of addiction. I was totally fooling myself.

The people who cared about me had no idea about my secret drug use. I wanted to be able to relax with a drink or two without alcohol becoming a problem, and the drugs were key to that. I knew enough about the body's biochemistry and the drugs I was taking to avoid any potential dangers—at least, that's what I told myself. I was a doctor, someone who saves lives. How could I misuse prescription drugs? Heck, I wrote prescriptions for other people because I knew so much about drugs and their dangers. That's how I saw it—Steve Heird, MD, couldn't possibly mess up in that department.

Despite my medical school training, no one ever told me that someone with an addiction can be highly functional and successful. That lesson was about to be learned through a lot of emotional pain and shame. When I sat across from my oldest son in our family room and had to tell him I would need to miss one of his important tennis matches, *and* his high school graduation in order to go into rehab, I felt overwhelmed with shame and self-loathing. How could I have screwed up so badly? I had hurt the people I loved most. Even today, I choke up just thinking about that horrible moment. I wouldn't wish it on anybody.

But having my secret revealed and going into rehab became a turning point. Sometimes, you need the universe to bring you what seems like a disaster in order to get to where you need and deserve to be. It was a long haul to get here, but now I feel a sense of fulfillment that I was grasping for all my life until my world came crashing down on me and I began to rebuild it. The hole in my soul, where a bitter north wind blew, could begin to heal. I learned how to feel whole and relaxed without drugs and alcohol. I discovered that the incredible feeling of freedom, joy, and power I got when skiing down a mountain, the cool and crisp air filling my lungs, was something I could experience every day. I still exercised and skied to meet my need for an adrenaline rush, but now I had some balance in my life. I started to read more—books that inspired me. And I changed the nature of my work so I could enjoy watching one of my children at a tennis match, basketball game, or ballet recital without worrying that I'd miss the next one because someone would need me to do surgery.

As I began to free myself from addictive thinking and behavior, I began to realize that happiness didn't have to disappear like a cloud of morning fog that lifts as soon as the sun starts to rise in the sky. I could hold on to it. I became content with simply being present in the moment. And in that moment, I reconnected with my sense of purpose and my childhood desire to be a healer.

In time, I realized that exactly how that goal manifested could change, and I could be the one to change the way I healed others. I recognized that I could lose my entire vascular surgery practice—and in fact, I did—but go on to build a new healing practice that was more in synch with who I am and how I want to help people today.

This book is an extension of my new commitment to living according to my purpose in this lifetime. In AA I learned that by listening to other people's stories of falling down and getting back up, I could gain insights about my own experience. I felt a sense of hope that like them, I too could rebuild my life. I hope that's what you get out of reading my story. Each of us has a different journey, but our paths can be more similar than we think. Your challenge might not be an addiction to drugs and alcohol but a softer addiction—maybe to working, shopping, or exercising. Maybe your challenge isn't an addiction but a sense of having to earn other people's love and approval. Discovering that I don't have to do anything to prove my self-worth was a huge and liberating revelation to me. I let go of burdens I didn't even know I was carrying. And did that feel good!

As you read my story, I hope you're entertained by some of my antics as a hyperactive kid turned adventurous adult. But I also hope that if addiction or low self-worth has hijacked your soul, you'll find hope in these pages. I really believe that every one of us can find a way to reconnect with our spirit and let go of the addictive thinking that distracts us from our truth. We just have to face our fears and open up to help from the universal Spirit. It's the first step that's the hardest one, but is it ever worth taking!

Chapter One

Snapshot of
a Perfect Life

T he Christmas tree upstairs in the family room and the one downstairs in the finished basement were now fully decorated. Why have one tree when you can have two? My wife, Dale, and I were in our storage space going through the presents we'd bought for the kids while the boys were at school and our three-year-old daughter was happily playing in her room. As usual, we had overbought. The piles were enormous. Since all three of my sons have January birthdays, and every year we went a little too crazy at the mall, we found ourselves once again pulling gifts to set aside to give them on their birthdays. After all, we didn't want to spoil them too much all in one day.

We had finished all our shopping with time to spare, and I was gearing up to cook for an entire day in anticipation of Dale's family coming over to celebrate. I was working long hours as a vascular surgeon in my booming practice, but I would have a couple of days off before seeing clients for consultation and follow-up and doing scheduled surgeries. The office was a mere ten-minute drive from home, and the hospital a few minutes' drive further down the road, so I was fortunate to save a lot of commuting time that I could spend doing projects around the house, going to my kids' special events, and taking afternoon runs with our dog, Brandy, trotting along beside me. There were days when I was so tired I'd come home and plop fully clothed on my bed, but Brandy would come into the bedroom, whimper, and give me that big-eyed look that he knew I couldn't resist. I'd change into my jogging clothes and shoes and take him outside for a five-mile run through the tree-lined streets of our suburban neighborhood. It was sunny even in the winter, and there were plenty of neighbors who would toot their horns or say hi to me as I passed.

Every Thanksgiving or Christmas, there was an abundance of food in the house. In fact, there was an abundance of everything in my life. All my relatives got along. The kids were doing great in school. We had established family traditions that we looked forward to every year, from the turkey or ham dinner to the fried oysters and shrimp cocktail on Christmas day. On Christmas Eve, Dale's parents would stop by in the afternoon, and we'd drink whiskey sours and have a few appetizers before heading off to Mass. We'd have a sit-down dinner, and after the plates were cleared, the kids would get to open one gift each before the end of the night.

Every year, it seemed there was some toy or piece of sporting equipment I had to assemble down in the family room, squinting at the instructions into the early hours of the morning while my wife slept and my kids dreamed about Santa's visit. No matter how excited they were the next morning, we all waited for everyone to wake up and gather by the tree before ripping the colorful gifts open and littering the rug with scraps of ribbon and paper.

The boys were growing older now and the ten and twenty dollar gifts from the toy store had given way to CDs, sports equipment, and clothes they thought would look cool on them. They had long since waged a rebellion against Dale's insistence that they dress alike and have similar haircuts for the family Christmas photo. My daughter's eyes grew wide at all the pink and purple toys we had chosen for her. I thought about what her Christmas day would be like if we had not found her through the adoption agency and brought her home to be part of our family. Being able to give her everything a little girl could want was a blessing. And having her was the biggest blessing. I was starting to get used to being a dad to a little girl. Loving my daughter felt different somehow from loving my sons. It was a unique and special feeling. She taught me that love absolutely transcends heredity. She has always felt like my own little girl.

The day after Christmas, all of us, including Dale's parents, would head out to my parents' house in the afternoon, and my brother and his wife and stepsons would join us. All the in-laws got along, and it was great that the cousins could spend time together.

I was always glad that Christmas meant my boys would get an entire week off from school. I spent as much time with them as I could when school was in session, but it was great to have them relaxed and hanging out with their friends during the day and then spend evenings with them after I got home from work. The hectic schedule we had was light that week—the boys' sports teams were usually on hiatus—and I got to take a break from my usual chauffeuring job.

And my vacations? I rarely took time just for myself. In fact, by this point, I was pretty much always working or squeezing in a short vacation with my wife and kids. Once in a while, we got to go skiing, which we all loved, but it had been a few years since I'd been able to fit in a week of helicopter skiing by myself. It's an extreme sport, not for the faint of heart or young children. Helicopter skiing was the one activity that was just for me, just for my enjoyment.

Whenever I went helicopter skiing, I felt fully alive. My adrenaline would pump through me, and I felt like all the weight of my responsibilities was lifted. I could zip down those mountain snow bowls and passes like an Olympian. Originally, going helicopter skiing was supposed to be a one-time adventure for me, but as my wife pointed out, my "one-time" adventure morphed into a once-a-year getaway—at least until the demands of my work and my parenting prevented me from doing it annually.

To go helicopter skiing had been a lifelong dream. The first time I did it was in Nakusp, British Columbia. I was going to take one week where I would be free from running the kids around and trying to juggle surgeries, follow-ups, and appointments. I finally had enough partners in my practice to feel confident that I wouldn't be called in to do an emergency surgery, cutting my vacation short. Up to that point, the danger of a ruptured aneurysm, which could kill a post-operative patient, made me afraid to go too far away from York.

When I got to the lodge we would start out from, they fitted me with an emergency transmitter so I could be found if there were an avalanche, and gave us a short training in how to do a search should that unusual event occur. We were told the biggest danger we were likely to face would be falling into a tree well: a circle of snow about three feet wide around an evergreen tree where the snow wouldn't accumulate, having been caught on the way down by the needles and branches. If you got too close, you'd fall into one of these holes head first. And if you panicked and struggled, the snow would fall on top of you and you'd suffocate. That was enough to sober you up and scare you off—unless you were me. The warning just made the whole experience more exciting as far as I was concerned. Oh, and you have to crouch a bit when entering and exiting the helicopter so the chopper's blades don't behead you. That could ruin the day for a lot of people looking forward to their day of expensive helicopter skiing.

We all followed the directions to stay away from tree wells and not to cross the trail blazed by the guide and risk falling off the cliff—that, too, would mess up the ski day. Like he instructed, we cut tracks to the right of the guide. I relished the sense of turning into the deep powder and having it spray against my face. It's like being in free fall. There's a rhythm to the turns, and you feel you're at one with the mountain. It's such a rush that you can't help but scream and hoot and holler—at least, I can't. I would guess for some people there would be screams of terror. The sport is definitely not for everyone.

I also love the moment when you've skied in to your spot near the little red flag they plant as your marker so the helicopter can meet your group easily. You're absolutely sweaty, you're covered in powder, and it's melting down the back of your neck, but you don't care because you're sweating anyway. Everyone is totally pumped and high-fiving, thrilled that there's yet another run. At the end of the day, you're dropped off at a lodge where you chow down on some barbecue spareribs and other appetizers before taking a plate and heading for the gourmet buffet line. There's also a physical therapist for massage therapy and a guided stretch, a hot tub, and a sauna. Believe me, you need all that to be able to get up again the next morning and push your muscles to do it all over again.

One year, at Christmas time in 2002, they had a light rain that formed thick ice on the surface of the snow. Over the next month, they had four feet of snow fall on top of that. The layer of ice from Christmas created instability whenever the temperature would get to the freezing point.

The guides all have avalanche training. They dig snow pits to check for the stability of snow. They even do dynamite runs with the helicopter to make sure that the snow was stable. In the back of the helicopter was a box of dynamite, and the guide would pull off a stick of it, remove the cap, light it, and toss it out of the helicopter at a spot in the snow. We'd hear the explosions, and he would observe the blasts and the aftermath to make sure that everything was okay. The guides knew about all the most stable spots that hadn't had an avalanche, even with the dynamite tossing, for decades, so I felt the risk was pretty slim. Getting caught up in an avalanche would definitely mess up the ski day.

On this particular Saturday, it was about one o'clock in the afternoon and we were taking the last ski run for the week. British Columbia had already experienced a major avalanche in which a famous snowboarder and other skiers had perished. On the mountain we would be skiing, the conditions weren't ideal in terms of avalanche safety, but all skiers and guides were being extra cautious as a result of that snow pack.

The temperature was just getting up to about zero degrees centigrade or 32 Fahrenheit, which we knew would make for dangerous conditions because of the Christmas rain turned to ice. Our group of ten flew into a bowl above the tree line that they had been using for many, many years and had never been a problem. We landed, we got our skis on, and the helicopter flew off to ferry another group.

The bowl was about 500 yards across—just a beautiful ridge that funneled down about 1,000 feet to a flat area at the next ridge. We had started down with our guide, Tom, in the front, and I got into one of those rhythms where you can do figure eights with another skier. It was bliss, really. And then I heard the guide shout, "Avalanche!" I turned to the right to see if anything had happened behind me, I didn't see a shifting of the snow in front of me. Then, I turned to the left and saw there was a fracture line in the bowl 500 yards wide. Four feet of snow was suddenly moving down the mountain to our left into our path. Of course, we immediately stopped skiing. In awe, we watched the wall of four feet of snow funnel down into this canyon area below us. It accumulated to 30 feet deep and then just pushed itself down the mountain for a half mile, blowing snow upward as the avalanche descended.

Tom radioed the helicopter and instructed the pilot, "Don't bring the next group in. We've had an avalanche, but everyone's okay."

I could hear the pilots say, "Roger. Do you need anything?"

"No," said Tom. "Just bring me a clean pair of underwear."

He understood the danger a lot better than I did. It reminded me that the snow, when it's moving like that, is full of air, but when the avalanche stops, the air escapes and the powder sets like concrete. If you're in it, you get crushed.

We skied over the firmly packed powder created by the avalanche and four-foot blocks of snow that had come down the mountain with it. As I felt it beneath my skis, I recognized that it was rock hard.

We were fortunate. That was not the case at Roger's Pass, which was over the mountain ridge. There was a school group from Calgary that had seventeen skiers back-country skiing: fourteen kids and three adults supervising. All but three were buried in the snow. From those fourteen, they pulled seven survivors. We learned about that as we were returning to Calgary. The president of the helicopter skiing company told us that they had sent helicopters to help with the rescue, and said it was important for us to contact our families immediately to let them know we had not been in the group caught in the avalanche. Then he added, "By the way, the Space Shuttle just exploded on re-entry over Texas."

That was the day the Columbia disintegrated. In the United States the news of the avalanche and the loss of life did not really make news like it would have otherwise because the Columbia disaster took the headlines. Whenever that event is mentioned, I remember my own brush with death.

Despite that incident, I went heli-skiing again, and plan to in the future. If I were to die heli-skiing, at least I'd die with a smile on my face.

Maybe I'm a little crazy having that as a hobby, but I can't help it. I always loved to be physically active and play sports. Sitting in a lounge chair by a pool or a beach and reading a novel was never my idea of a good time. That was my wife's thing. The last long vacation I'd taken with her was ten years before. Her parents had offered to babysit our three boys, including the youngest, who was just an infant, while Dale and I went skiing. Unfortunately, my surgery partner went ahead and booked a two-week vacation in Hawaii at a time-share without telling me. When I realized our dates would overlap, I asked him to cancel his plans. After all, I'd had mine for almost eighteen months. He didn't want to, and figured if anyone needed emergency surgery while we were both gone, they could go to our competitor. But I just couldn't accept that. I didn't want to let anyone down, and I didn't think our competitor was as good a surgeon as we were. Since my partner wouldn't budge, I lost the $500 deposit at the ski resort. Dale and I booked a short cruise instead. It was the logical solution.

The fact that I really wanted to go skiing didn't factor into it for me. I didn't want to upset my new partner by pushing him harder to cancel his vacation. Dale and I ended up booking a three-night, four-day Caribbean cruise together, which meant I could be back working on patients without the practice suffering.

Soon, I was on an excursion boat in the waters off of St. John's feeling the warm tropical breeze against my skin and looking down through impossibly turquoise water to the ripples of sand at the bottom of the ocean as we traveled out to snorkel at a coral reef, where we could immerse ourselves in a living tropical fish tank. What's not to like? But even as my wife said, "Oh, this is a dream come true!" I felt a heaviness in my gut. I flashed her a smile and she gazed back at the water again, completely unaware of what I was really feeling and thinking: If only I were skiing!

Dale started talking to me about something and I distracted myself, trying to listen to what she was saying, but my feeling that this wasn't what I wanted lingered. My resistance would go away soon, that much I knew. I was good at distracting myself from my feelings. I'd become used to letting thoughts like *I wish...* and *you know, what I'd like is...* slip out of my mind.

Distraction can be good. It means having a thirst for novelty—and challenge. It means being creative. I strongly suspect I have ADHD, which incorporates all of those things. But despite the "deficit" in Attention Deficit Hyperactivity Disorder, I don't have trouble paying attention to what's really important to me. When I try to concentrate on my son's tennis serve and whether his opponent can return the lobby, or I focus on doing surgery to repair abdominal aortic aneurysms, my mind's like a laser beam. "Work hard, play hard" had been my motto since I was a teen. Whatever I choose to direct my laser-like focus to holds my attention. I credit my successes to that focus along with dogged perseverance, creativity when I come up against an obstacle, and a natural curiosity. I couldn't deny that the way I operated led me to create a picture perfect family and life.

But a snapshot can be deceiving. I have plenty of pictures of that cruise I took with Dale. I look happy standing there on the deck of the ship, or toasting the camera with a bottle of beer. Inside, though, there was a restlessness that no tropical breeze was going to sweep away and no night drinking, talking, and laughing was going to fix. At home, even hauling in thousands of dollars in a matter of hours as I did back-to-back and perfect surgeries didn't make that restlessness go away. I had figured out plenty of ways to distract myself from that emptiness, but I sure didn't spend any time thinking about it, much less confiding in anyone how I felt.

And then, one day, the universe conspired to rip up the snapshot and smash the camera. That perfect life came to an end with a phone call.

Chapter Two

My Secret
Is Out

There, behind the pile of sweaters on the shelf of my bedroom closet, was my secret that I hid well from everyone, especially from my wife. She had no way of knowing that a few small vials—Vicodin and Valium, maybe some Tylenol with codeine or Soma with codeine—that bore her name and the logo of one of four local pharmacies were nestled behind that stack of clothing. As far as I was concerned, she would never catch me, and neither would anyone else. When the vials emptied, I was careful to dispose of them discreetly.

The first time I filled the prescription I had written for Dale but intended to use myself, I took it to a local pharmacy on a sleepy Sunday. I was in my car at the drive-through when suddenly a pharmacist I knew socially popped his head out of the window, startling me.

"Steve! How are you doing?" he said in his usual friendly way.

I can't believe he works here! I tried to be as casual as can be as I said hello. We filled each other in on our kids as I waited for the bag with the receipt stapled to it.

"These are for your wife, then?"

"Yes," I said without hesitation. How did that lie come to me so easily? This was the first time I had faked a prescription. My wife had absolutely no idea I was taking prescription drugs, much less that I would deceive someone to attain them. I couldn't explain to her that to keep up my frenetic pace, and retain my habit of having a beer or two at night after a long day's work without nodding off, I needed to take them.

Years before when I was in medical school, I had dabbled with drugs like marijuana and even cocaine, but they were never a big part of my life. As my pace picked up during the three years I was building my practice, I started using prescription painkillers here and there at first. I tried out the samples the drug representatives left in my office. After all, I felt I should have a sense of their effect on the body. I discovered I liked the sensation they gave me. They made me feel more energized, at least for a few hours.

I was too busy to sit down and have a beer, but the pills gave me quick relief from the feelings I didn't want to feel. The stress of my responsibilities as a surgeon, father, and spouse often weighed me down. The drugs gave me a much needed break from that stress. In medical school and even more so later when I was a resident, I learned to suck it up and push my body and my mind through sleeplessness and weariness. I was taught that it was weak to admit I had limits to what I could get done in a day or a week. Taking it a little easier just wasn't an option.

Slowly, my usage increased. Soon, I found I could go without the drugs for a few days, but I was afraid of how exhausted I would feel if I didn't take them. I believed I just had to get this prescription filled until some more samples came in. It would be just this one time. I had patients counting on me. My family was counting on me. I didn't want to fall asleep after work when my sons had a tennis match or basketball game, and I knew that could happen as the effects of the painkillers wore off. No, it would be just this one time—at least, that's what I told myself. I won't get addicted. Every addict remembers saying that, and believing it.

At the drive-through window that day, my friend the pharmacist said, "It'll be just a minute. Percocet is a Class 2 narcotic, so I have to file a report with the state board that I just filled this prescription."

"No problem," I said. *Bad choice,* I thought. *Vicodin is a Class 3 narcotic. I'll bet they don't keep track of Vicodin prescriptions. I'll have to look it up.*

Sure enough, Vicodin prescriptions could be filled without any authoritative body being notified. And Percocet, also known by its generic name OxyContin, is more addictive than Vicodin is. So a few months later, when I inevitably decided I couldn't wait to receive more Vicodin samples from the pharmaceutical company, I wrote another prescription for Dale—this one, for Vicodin. I was silently thankful that she had a man's name so that when I took the prescription to a different pharmacy, if the druggist looked at "Dale Heird" on the label and asked, "Is this for you, then?" I could say, "Yes."

In time, as my addiction grew stronger, I started to make the rounds of several different pharmacies. It wasn't hard to do because I was running the kids to sporting events all over the county, so I had plenty of choices of drugstores. The stress of keeping track of which ones I had used most recently was piling up, but what could I do? Now, I was taking the drugs daily, first thing in the morning. I'd pop another after work to perk me up, and then drink a beer or two to take the edge of the jitters they created. The buzz I felt after that was perfect. I only did it on vacation or days off when I wasn't on call—at least, at first.

But my addiction was taking its toll. I couldn't feel normal in the morning without the drugs. I was starting to operate while on drugs, but I was completely convinced that with my laser-sharp focus and high level of skills, I was fine. Every patient sailed through the surgery perfectly. I had an incredible track record. I figured I could take the pills when I was on call "just this one time." As my withdrawal symptoms increased, I convinced myself that if the worst case happened and I had to do an emergency surgery while on Vicodin, I could get through it just fine.

My family didn't suspect anything. Sometimes, I would nod off at dinner or at parties. The problem is I would take the drugs so as not to drink too much at the party, which I was prone to do because I tend to be uncomfortable going to social events. It's not that I'm shy, but alcohol made me gregarious despite my insecurities. The mixing of alcohol and prescription drugs would make me sleepy. My falling asleep embarrassed my wife to the point where she stopped wanting to go out. That bothered me a lot, but I didn't feel I could do anything about it—except take the prescription drugs to keep me alert.

The thing about addiction is you know that you're doing things you shouldn't, and you care about it. You feel ashamed and remorseful. Yet you also feel powerless to do anything. You wonder, "What's wrong with me?" Because there's no clear answer, you just talk yourself into believing you can choose to stop the substance abuse at any time. *Tomorrow would be a good option*—that's what you think. *I'll stop tomorrow.*

For me, drinking was a relief from the guilt, shame, remorse, and powerlessness. The only really scary moment was when I fell asleep at the wheel for a second while driving my kids somewhere while their friends were in the car. Instantly, they shouted at me, and I woke up and pulled over. The adrenaline shooting through my system and my racing heart woke me up right away. It was only one time, but it scared me. I wish I could say it scared me enough to tell myself, "I have a problem and I have to do something." Unfortunately, even though I knew there was a problem, my fear was so great that I couldn't bring myself to ask for help. My wife and kids figured I was tired from working so many hours and sleeping so little. I decided to latch on to that explanation for my momentary nap behind the wheel rather than face the truth. I've always been able to get by on four or five hours of sleep a night, ever since I was a kid, so I knew that sleep deprivation wasn't the issue. Still, overwork was an acceptable excuse for misjudging just how tired I was that day when I fell asleep when driving, so I went with it. That's addictive thinking for you. There's always a ready excuse. There's always a rationale that will silence that little voice that says, "This can't be right. Maybe I have a problem…"

The morning the DEA agents approached me had started like most mornings. I took a shower, secretly popped a Vicodin to control my withdrawal symptoms, replaced the vial behind the sweater pile, and headed off to work. The day before, I had done a major surgical procedure repairing five aneurysms in one patient. An aneurysm is very serious enlargement of the artery that can be life threatening, but the patient had come through brilliantly. Today, my first task was to get myself over to the hospital to check on him. He was in the ICU recovering with a breathing tube still inserted, which is normal with these types of surgery. I was in my suit, ready to get back to the office, switch into my scrubs, and do half a dozen back-to-back procedures for a string of patients who had appointments that day. My ICU patient was doing well and all his numbers and tests looked good. I told him I was going to check on his X-rays and headed off for the radiology department.

As soon as I got through the door, my beeper went off. I could see it was my home number. Dale rarely called me at work, so I wanted to get back to her right away as it had to be important. Cell phone use wasn't allowed in the hospital—they were afraid cell phones would interfere with monitoring equipment—so my only option was to pick up the phone in the room to return the call.

"What's up?" I asked.

"Um, Steve? What's this about narcotics?"

My heart began to race and my mouth grew dry.

Dale continued, "I just got out of the shower and went to answer the doorbell, and it was two DEA agents. I told them I'd have to talk to them some other time, but they were really insistent. So I let them in. But the whole thing was pretty intimidating. I mean, I'm standing there in nothing but a bathrobe! They started asking about narcotics, and I told them I have no idea what they were talking about. They're gone now. But what was that about?"

"You signed something?" I said it as softly as possible, turning my back to the nurse and radiation technician who were in the room looking at X-rays and talking with each other.

"They put a paper underneath my nose," she continued, "and said, 'Sign this if you don't know anything about narcotics and you didn't take narcotic prescriptions written for you.' So I did. Then, they said they're coming to talk to you and told me not to tell you. What's going on?"

"I'm addicted to painkillers. I need help, and I'm in trouble."

There. I had said it. I had finally spoken the truth that I'd been holding back, even from myself—seemingly forever.

"You're in trouble? Wh—what are you saying?"

"I'm saying I'm in trouble. You just signed a paper saying I'm guilty of illegal activities—that's what that was. They're going to put me in jail."

She was silent, trying to process what I had just said.

I took a breath. "I've been writing illegal prescriptions. Some of them are in your name. That's what this is about. You just signed a piece of paper committing me to being guilty because you just admitted the drugs weren't for you."

"Oh God, Steve. I screwed up." I could hear the worry in her voice. "Now I got you into more trouble. I should have kicked them out of the house. Or checked before I answered the door and called you. Oh God!"

"It's okay. I mean, the reality of it is I need help." As I said it, a felt a surge of relief descend upon me. The secret was out. Calmness overtook me. The tension that had been in my muscles for months—no, actually, years—was finally lifting.

That's not to say I knew what to do. The truth is I didn't know what was wrong with me. In those rare moments when I thought about what was happening to me, I was aware that I was addicted to painkillers. The signs of physical addiction were unmistakable. If I didn't take them, I would experience muscle aches, a runny nose, restless legs, and agitation. What I didn't understand was why I had let it get this far. Every time I tried to figure out what happened, I short-circuited my thought process, because it never got me to any answers.

I wasn't trying to get high by taking painkillers. I was just trying to function. For years, I had enjoyed social drinking and a little pot smoking—and that was mostly in the 70s when it seemed every long-haired guy was enjoying the occasional joint. And everyone drank beer after work like I was doing, right? I had a good life, and a reasonably good childhood. I was successful. I was a doctor who knew the dangers of addiction. None of it added up to an explanation that made any sense.

I had no idea how powerful denial could be. I would stop taking the drugs, suffer the withdrawal symptoms, yet push through them until the medications had cleared my system completely. Then, within a week or two, I'd have a couple of beers and get the idea to pop a pill again—"just this once." I'm a smart, rational person, but my thinking was completely distorted. How could that be? I wondered. I just couldn't understand why I would return to the drugs. In AA, they say "it is stinking thinking that keeps you drinking"—or in my case, drinking and drugging.

The addiction had crept up on me. It was insidious and baffling. Now, I finally felt relief and being unburdened of my secret. But at the same time, I was scared. What would happen now? I didn't quite understand the severity or gravity of the situation yet. I just knew that I had to think.

The practice had just started doing vein treatments, and I had patients in my waiting room at the office. I was slated to make more money that day than I had ever made on a day of surgery. What was I going to do about their treatments?

It really wasn't losing the money that bothered me, though. It was cancelling the appointments and disappointing and inconveniencing my patients. I thought, *if I don't take care of my patients, they'll be angry with me.* A feeling of shame and inadequacy started to rise within me. All my life, I'd felt the need to be seen as reliable, nice guy who would help everyone out. I wanted to be looked up to, and loved. Everyone saw me as that nice guy you can always count on. They had no idea I'd been carrying this secret.

What would my patients think of me? What would my parents think about me?

I definitely didn't want to think about that. My mom and dad had always been supportive of me, even when I was having trouble getting the grades and test scores that would earn me a place in an American medical school. They believed in me.

I felt a driving need to get to the office and get to my patients. After that—well, I'd figure it out after the treatments had been completed. I told myself that this other stuff, as big as it seemed to be, wasn't big enough to lose my focus. What mattered now were my patients.

How would my boys react? What would my wife say when I got home?

My thoughts were about everybody but me. I had a problem that I needed to focus on but all I could think about was damage control so that I could minimize my family's hurt.

"What do I do, Steve?"

I could hear the fear in my wife's voice. "I'll let you know what's going on later. I have to get to the office. I'll call you back as soon as I can."

I took a deep breath or two to calm my nerves as I made my way to the parking lot, intending to drive to the office about five minutes away. Just as I was about to step into my car, my secretary called.

"Dr. Heird, there are two agents here to speak to you. What should I tell them?"

My brain went on autopilot. "Well, I've got a really busy day. We have all these people to take care of. I'm too busy to talk to any agents. Find out when I can contact them and tell them I'll speak to them another time. Send them away, please."

I actually thought that the agents would buy my logic and recognize that I was a very important physician in the community, give my secretary their card, and go away, leaving me to carry on with my everyday business. I still didn't understand they wanted me. I thought they were just gathering information. I got in my car and continued with my agenda for the day.

I was about 500 yards away from the parking lot for the medical center where my office is located when my cell phone rang again.

"Dr. Heird," said my secretary, a hint of worry in her voice, "I told those agents to go away, but I don't think they left. I think they're waiting for you in the parking lot."

Uh oh. This is bad. In an instant, I pulled into the parking lot where my barber worked, did a U-turn, and began driving back in the other direction. *They want me. They know I'm using drugs.* I glanced in the rearview mirror and hit my turn signal. "Thank you. I'm not coming to work today. Cancel all my appointments." I sounded calm but inside, I was turning to jelly. *What do I do?*

Then, out of some recess in my brain, a memory of the TV show "NYPD Blue" came to me. *The detectives hate it when the perps lawyer up. You've gotta lawyer up.*

I pulled over again, the voice becoming more insistent. *Lawyer up, Steve.*

I called my wife and said, "The agents are at my office, waiting in the parking lot."

"They told me they were going straight there. I'm sorry. I thought you were still at the hospital. They told me not to tell you they were going to try to meet you."

"It's okay," I said. She had sort of warned me. It's not as if she was practiced at tipping off her husband to the movements of DEA agents.

I couldn't emotionally process what was happening. I had always relied on my wits to get me out of sticky situations and that's what this was. But suddenly, an idea came to me. "I'm headed to our attorney's office."

Chapter Three   Closing In

T he reality of what was going on was just beginning to set in and true fear was starting to grab hold of me. What had I done? My mind was racing. I'd never known someone in this situation so I had no idea what I was facing, but it was clear to me that I was in very big trouble. At the same time, I felt, "Oh, my God, I am finally going to get help for this dreadful secret that I have been keeping to myself for so long." Fear and relief battled each other.

For years, I had denied my addiction and my sense of powerlessness over it. I'd been making excuses to myself for why I was unable to stop drinking and taking the pills. They gave me relief from the pressures of my life, but beyond that, I couldn't explain it to myself, much less to anyone who might find out how bad my compulsions had gotten.

I was aware that by telling Dale I'm addicted to painkillers and I need help, I had made my first honest statement about the situation. Even as I said it, I felt an energetic shift in myself, as if I had stepped into a new reality.

I was so discombobulated that I gave Dale the name of the wrong attorney, someone we knew socially but hadn't worked with. Even so, she guessed that I was actually driving to the office of David, our attorney who had prepared the paperwork when we were applying to adopt our daughter. I drove north on South George Street a few blocks, and then pulled into the small parking lot behind David's office just as he was pulling up to begin his work day.

I stepped out of my car and could feel myself shaking from nerves. I thought that maybe the agents were now tailing me. Of course, they couldn't know where I had gone but it felt as if they were closing in. I thought, *they're going to arrest me. I'm in big, big trouble.*

David looked at me with surprise as soon as he got out of his car. We approached each other, and I said, "Hello, David. I'm sorry I didn't call, but I need your help. I'm addicted to painkillers. I've been writing illegal prescriptions, the Drug Enforcement Administration is after me, and they're trying to arrest me. Can you help me? Is there someplace safe I can go?"

He looked at me for just a moment before saying, "Yes. Come on inside. We can keep you in here, and you'll be safe. They can't arrest you here."

I felt some of the tension leave my body. Lawyering up had definitely been the right idea.

I followed him into the building and since my visit was unexpected, he had to take care of a few things before talking to me. He decided to have another attorney in his firm sit down in his conference room and interview me to gather information before joining me. David ushered me into the room and motioned for me to take a seat. He offered me coffee but I said no thanks. I was jumpy enough.

There was a long table, ten leather-covered wooden chairs, and bookshelves filled with important looking legal volumes. My mind reeled and churned and did somersaults as I waited for the other attorney to arrive.

A few minutes later, in walked Ms. Rodriguez. She was about forty and blonde, and looked every inch the professional. She had a soothing, gentle voice and asked me a lot of good questions. Before I knew it, was crying—not just sniffing or getting a little misty, but really crying. It might have been embarrassing but honestly, I just had so much fear, guilt, and anguish to release that I didn't have room inside me to feel embarrassment. I had years of shit packed inside me that I had to let go of—major league burdens. And I was scared of the legal consequences of what I'd done.

I was so distraught that I just let everything pour out. I didn't realize it at the time, but letting the tears flow was the first step in my healing process. I tried to focus on the fact that I was going to get help and trusted that Ms. Rodriguez and David would be able to get me out of this mess somehow.

I wasn't used to asking for help. I liked to think of myself as very self-sufficient. But knowing they had the ability to figure out my next move gave me a sense of faith that kept me from completely falling apart in that conference room. Despite my tears, I was able to tell Ms. Rodriguez all the details she needed. I even told her I had pills on me, in my pocket. I needed to keep them with me to control the withdrawal symptoms.

Addiction isolates you. The state of denial is a very lonely place. You feel separate from spirit and from other people that you're convinced will judge you and reject you. When you think about how alone you feel despair sets in. The only solution is to keep doing what you've been doing to experience the relief from that despair and fear once again. The drugs give you a temporary sense of freedom from your fears. As I sat there telling my story and answering questions, I realized this was the first time in a very long time I didn't feel isolated and alone.

After an hour or so, David came back in and sat down next to me. "I'll tell it to you straight, Steve. Your activities, what the Drug Enforcement Administration has been investigating, could result in the loss of your license. Now, your addiction is a medical issue. But, having written false prescriptions is a legal issue. That's what could cause you to lose your license."

"For how long?"

"Ten years."

I swallowed. *Ten years without a livelihood! What would I do?*

David's expression was serious, but not grim. "You've got some choices to make. Fraud is a felony, and they might press criminal charges, so you'll need an attorney to handle the legal issue of your license. You'll also need someone who can defend you in a criminal case. I have some names for you."

When I looked at his list, I saw the name Joshua Lock—yes, that was actually his last name!—who had offices in Harrisburg. That's about 25 miles north of York. That sounded good to me, especially since I had a compelling urge to get out of town. I asked about him, and David said, "He's high profile. And he can represent you on both fronts."

"That sounds perfect," I said.

David called Lock's office and made an appointment for me at 4:00 p.m. Then, he gave me a list of rehab centers to call. I didn't realize it until he confided in me later, but he had a close family member that went through rehab for addiction. He knew that I would have to go into an inpatient program immediately.

I surrendered to David's plan. What else could I do? I had to trust in someone. I couldn't do this without good legal advice. I said good-bye to the kind Ms. Rodriguez, and then hurried out the door to my car. I still had the feeling that somehow those DEA agents were right behind me, ready to jump out and slap handcuffs on me.

There was a chance of going to jail and the potential to lose everything that I had spent a lifetime working for. But that wasn't all. I feared I would lose my family, too.

I thought about my oldest son, Billy, who was a star tennis player. I had been traveling with him to several states to attend his tennis matches. He had just finished playing in the district tournament and was heading to a state tennis match. He had a chance to win the Pennsylvania state high school title as the best high school tennis player in the state of Pennsylvania. And I wasn't going to be there to watch him play in this all-important match. I knew I was going straight into rehab. And I was going to miss his high school graduation, which was coming up in a few weeks. I didn't know much about rehab, but I had heard that 28 days was the minimum stay.

From the car, I called my wife and told her what was happening. She asked what she should do, and I said, "I don't know. Maybe you should talk to our priest."

"Maybe I'll do that," she said.

It took about 45 minutes to drive to the building where Lock's office was in Strawberry Square, a well-landscaped walking mall across from the state capital building. When I arrived, it was only a little after 11:00 a.m., so I just went up to the office to let them know I was there. The receptionist, Jill, was tall, attractive, and impeccably dressed. Her confidence began to shift my nervous energy—not so much because of what she said, as there wasn't much she could tell me at that point. But her voice was like honey as she suggested to me that I call my wife and have her drive up to meet me.

I thanked her and told her I'd kill time walking around outside. It was an incredible spring day, with the buds on the trees beginning to flower. Daffodils were already in bloom and tulips beginning to open. I tried phoning Dale several times to no avail, which made me feel even more isolated and lonely. Eventually, she answered and told me she had put her cell phone on "silent" because she was talking at length to our priest, as I'd suggested. She said she would have to get someone to help with the kids while she was out but yes, she would drive up to Harrisburg to meet me.

I hung up, feeling slightly better, and then walked around some more. At some point, I picked up some takeout to keep me going, but I wasn't very hungry for lunch. All I could think about was what was going to happen now. I was facing criminal charges. I was facing the loss of my medical license and my livelihood. Would my wife leave me? Would I lose our house? My practice? My family was going to be in shock, and then what would they think? Everything that I ever worked for might be lost. The thought was overwhelming, and I tried to distract myself by walking down this street, and then that one.

Finally, four o'clock arrived and I took the elevator up to Josh Lock's office.

His receptionist, Jill, had a calm, reassuring attitude I could appreciate as I sat there waiting for Josh Lock to call me into his office.

Within minutes, Dale arrived and joined me in the conference room. I filled her in, and she told me she had someone to watch our daughter and be there to get the boys dinner if we were very late getting back. She was being very practical and that helped me to calm my nerves. In retrospect, I was in shock, but I can remember feeling a sense of hope now that my secret was out. I was determined to turn this around and take a new path.

Josh Lock came in and introduced himself with a firm handshake, and my first impression was that he was very professional but friendly, too. He explained that he had represented many high profile clients in Pennsylvania and successfully defended them in criminal court.

"Any physicians?" I asked.

"Oh yes," he said. He explained that there was another lawyer in his office who did licensing work, primarily for dentists, but for some physicians as well. It was a big law firm and very expensive, but right away I could tell he was worth every penny I was going to pay him.

"Take care of yourself," said Josh. "Get into a rehab hospital immediately and get well. I'll contact the DEA's agents and ask them if they'll hold off on charging you with whatever it is they've got until you are out of the rehab hospital."

"You think I'll be okay?" I asked, hoping he'd rain reassurance on me.

"After I talk to the DEA, I'll have a feel for what the charges are that we're dealing with. There are absolutely no guarantees whatsoever, but we'll see what we can do. In cases similar to yours, we've had doctors lose their license. We've had people that have been able to complete a drug court program and have their criminal charges expunged, so now they have no criminal record whatsoever. There's a range of possible results."

So much for my hope of a promise that everything would be okay. In a sense, his honesty was reassuring, though. I was overdue for facing the truth, however harsh it was.

"I have to warn you, though," he said quietly. "The Attorney General of Pennsylvania is looking to become the governor in 2010, and he's already working on his campaign. Any publicity for him will be good publicity. He's sure to send out a press release about whatever charges it is that you face. I want you and your wife and children to start being aware of that, so that when it hits the media they'll be emotionally prepared to handle it."

I quickly glanced over at Dale. Appearances were important to her. We had a beautiful family. We had a beautiful home. And now, we would be the family whose father was facing criminal drug charges.

And what will my partners say? What will my patients think?

"Thanks for the heads up," I said to Josh. "That's it, then?"

"Yes," he told me, getting up. He shook my hand—then Dale's.

I said, "You know, I came all the way up here because David said you were terrific, and you are. But I also figured by going all the way to Harrisburg, I'd get away from those DEA agents."

He chuckled. "You didn't get very far. The attorney general's office is right here in this building."

I stared at him for a moment, dumbfounded.

"So, the agents are coming and going all the time. You came to them. You could've run into them on your way in!"

I laughed nervously. By now, I realized that they actually couldn't arrest me and take me away as long as I said, "I have no comment. Please contact my attorney, Josh Lock," as instructed. But the irony was still kind of shocking and as I left the building with Dale, my walking pace was just a bit more brisk than normal.

Dale got in her car and I got into mine to follow her home. As I drove, I left the radio off to be alone with my thoughts in the quiet. I was going to have an opportunity to get help at a rehabilitation hospital. Everything else could be addressed when I was out of rehab. I'd take the boys aside and explain everything. I'd find a simple way to explain it to my daughter, and hug her and tell her daddy was going to be okay, just gone for a while.

I swallowed. I didn't want to think about these scenes, or what Dale was thinking in the car ahead of me.

Josh had told me to contact a psychiatrist, Dr. Stefan, whom he had worked with on a case with a dentist who had gotten in trouble. He suggested that I get to know this doctor so that if I had to go to a trial, I might be able to call him as a character witness who could testify that I was earnest in wanting to get off of drugs and set things right. I'd give him a call later, after talking to the rehab centers to find out whether they took my insurance and whether I could get admitted right away.

As it turned out, I was able to find a rehabilitation facility a few hours away that could take me the next evening. I'd have a chance to talk to my kids before leaving. That was important to me. I wanted the news to come from me, not Dale.

I called Dr. Stefan next, and he gave me a very important piece of advice.

"The thing about doctors, Steve, is that we're smart. We know how to talk the talk, and fool people into thinking we're just fine when we aren't. The rehab will probably let you out after twenty-eight days, and then you'll crash and burn. You need to stay until you're really ready to leave—until you've done the work and gotten past your denial. Don't rush it."

I thought about how well I'd hidden my addiction, including from one of my professors in medical school who had called me in after a nurse reported smelling alcohol on my breath. I was good at talking fast and making good excuses for myself that a reasonable person would buy.

"I hear you," I said. "It's going to be hard to miss my son's tennis match and graduation… But I need to do this for myself. Now."

"You do. And Steve, by the way, my drug of choice was Percocet. And I've been sober for twenty years."

I let that settle in. Maybe someday I'd be like him, sober and able to offer advice and talk frankly about what happened to me. I wished I could leapfrog forward to that moment in time, but there was a lot of work ahead of me. I was just glad to be surrounded by people—strangers until today—willing to help me.

It was going to be a hard path, but I had pushed myself past obstacles before. I wasn't exactly destined to be a highly successful surgeon but I got it into my head that I wanted to be one and worked hard to reach my goal. Now, I'd made everything fall apart. But maybe I would be able to find it in me to reconstruct my life. I had to hold on to that hope.

That evening after I made all my phone calls and had a plan, I had a meeting with the kids and told them what had happened.

I took the three boys into the family room and asked them to sit down. I told them, "I messed up. I'm addicted to painkillers, and I've made some very bad choices. I'm facing some legal problems but I have a good lawyer, one of the best there is, so you don't have to worry about that. I'm going to a hospital tomorrow to get help from professionals and I'll be gone at least a month. Your mother's going to need some extra help. She might ask you to do some extra chores, or watch your sister."

"That's okay," they promised. "You can count on us." All of them had adjusted quickly to having a little sister, and the oldest two had even been happy to do diaper changes when she was still a toddler.

"I talked to grandma and grandpa and they said they can help out, too, if it's necessary." I swallowed hard. Telling my father had been a low point. He was supportive and kind, but it killed me to think how disappointed he must be.

I asked them if they had any questions and they said no, but then I looked at my oldest son and I could see what he was thinking. This was a very important time in his life and I wouldn't be there for him. I asked him to follow me to the basement on some pretense and told the other boys we could talk more later.

When we were alone, I said to Billy, "I'm so sorry. I'm not going to be able to come to your tournament but I know you can beat this kid."

"Yeah," he said. He was going up against a rival player who had bested him in the past, and I really wanted to be there in the stands cheering him on.

"I talked to Uncle Rusty. He can stand in for me at your graduation. I can't tell you how sorry I am. If there was any way…"

"It's okay, dad. I understand. This is important for you. You've gotta do what you've gotta do."

I nodded.

"You've been a good dad," he said.

In that moment, I realized that whatever I had to deal with, I had the reassurance of knowing I hadn't screwed up everything in my life. I had a son who had grown into a young man to be very proud of.

I had always been able to always focus on my children, no matter how stressed out I was or how uncomfortable I felt battling the side effects of the medications I was taking. My kids were my reason for living. I hadn't lost track of that despite everything. They were the source of my joy, and would continue to be. I was now starting to experience a ray of hope knowing that I was getting help and that feeling of fear and despair was going to be a thing of the past. I would make this up to Billy—to all of them—somehow.

That night, I was able to sleep with the help of some sleeping pills and Valium. I figured I might as well use them because otherwise, I would have withdrawal symptoms within a few hours. I didn't wash them down with a beer. The one I'd had the night before would be my last beer ever, although I didn't realize it at the time. I had what's known as a cross addiction to prescription drugs and alcohol. "Just a beer," I would learn in rehab, would send me right back into the addictive behaviors. The next morning, as I cleaned out my SUV in preparation for the trip to rehab, I was stunned at how many beer bottles were stuffed under the seats, in the door pockets, and in every nook and cranny of the vehicle. To them, I added pill vials I had secretly collected for disposal when I got the chance. The evidence of my addiction filled an entire garbage bag.

As I was packing, I heard a car pull up and glanced out the window. *The DEA agents.* Instinctively, I ran up the stairs and peeked out one of our dormers. Although I couldn't hear what the two men in khakis and polo shirts were saying to Dale, it was clear she was telling them firmly to go away. They got back into their car and drove off.

"What did they say?" I asked when I got back downstairs and she came in the back door.

"They asked if you were here and I said yes, but he's not going to talk to you—you'll have to talk to our attorney, Josh Lock. They said they knew him. And then, one of them said, 'Is your husband getting help?' And I said, 'Yes.' Then he said, 'Good.'"

"So I guess that's the end of them. If they know what's going on, they'll leave you alone while I'm gone."

She nodded.

I stood there for a moment, trying to think of what to say. What was there to say? Dale's a good person. She'd been pretty patient waiting for me to get through the crazy hours of my medical residency. She'd followed me from place to place, uprooting herself and letting dinner get cold when my work demanded that I stay at the hospital unexpectedly. She'd put up with the stress of my trying to build a practice, and my having to be on call most of the time while my partner and I looked for a third partner. Still, all my hard work and her support had taken us a long way. The life I'd created for myself wasn't one you'd expect of a kid who was a turkey farmer's son.

Chapter Four

The Turkey Farmer's Son

U nlike a lot of surgeons, I didn't come from a long line of doctors and college graduates. Neither of my parents went to college, and together they ran a turkey farm.

My mother grew up on a farm in Hampstead, Maryland, with two older brothers and a younger sister. It was her grandfather's family farm, and her father and his eight siblings had all grown up there, too. When I was born, a few years after my brother Jesse, who went by the nickname Rusty, I was named Steve and given the middle name Buchman, after my mom's family.

My father's side of the family was much smaller. His father, who was much older than my paternal grandmother, died when my dad was 14. Dad's older sister, my Aunt Eleanor, ended up living with grandma in a small house in Manchester, Maryland, struggling to make ends meet. During the Depression, grandma worked for seventeen cents an hour in a sewing factory to keep food on the table so her two kids could remain in school. I heard that story many times when I asked my parents for pocket money! Anyway, both dad and aunt Eleanor did graduate from high school, as did my mom. But dad went on to work in an airplane assembly factory, got drafted as a World War II paratrooper, went back to factory work, and then become a turkey farmer. He could have gone to college on the GI Bill because he was a paratrooper, but he used the money instead to get pilot training. It had always been his dream to own and fly a plane, and thanks to the GI Bill, he was able to do that.

My mom missed out on a higher education for a different reason. She had been accepted at Western Maryland College in Westminster, Maryland, but graduated from high school in 1943, right in the middle of World War II. People considered it unpatriotic for a woman to go to college when companies were crying out for female workers to fill in for the men who were off at the front. Mom was hired by the local bank, but never got over her disappointment at ending her education at high school. She dreamed that someday, her sons would be able to attend and graduate from college. My dad didn't have his heart set on seeing us become college grads, but he worked very hard on the farm. He was extremely successful, but I think he might have wanted an easier life for his sons.

Whatever her teenage aspirations might have been, mom became a dedicated farmer's wife who made sure there were three square meals on the table at 7:30 a.m., noon, and 5:00 p.m. We all sat down together at breakfast and dinner, and at lunchtime if my brother and I weren't at school.

There were always plenty of animals around, from cats and dogs to cows and ponies, but it was the turkeys that put the money in the bank. My dad switched over to chickens when I was fourteen, and at one point we had 68,000, but when I was a kid, it was all turkeys. Dad had just one full-time employee, Lawrence, most of the year, but for those ten days or so of slaughtering season which was just before Thanksgiving and just before Christmas, he had to hire up to fifteen part-time employees to help him slaughter and prepare 900 turkeys a day. It was a lucrative business but very stressful for him because he could never be sure if he would be able to hire enough reliable workers, if the weather would cooperate, or if he would succeed in getting the turkeys to market in time for the two big holidays to recoup his huge investment in them. Later, around the time I entered high school, he decided to convert to chicken farming, which provided reliable income from eggs all year and wasn't so stressful during the holidays. He was a lot less irritable after that.

But when I was younger and he was raising turkeys, I sensed my father's constant worry and fear that something would go wrong. There was a sense of lack, despite the abundance that surrounded us. The way they lived was a reflection of the Depression, when mom and dad were growing up. Back in those days, there was no credit, and farmers lost their land when the banks called in their loans. The insecurity of that time made a deep impression on my parents. My father's grandfather literally did lose the farm—a 175-acre one—after the 1929 market crash. My great-grandfather and great-grandmother became homeless and had to move in with relatives. Wherever they went, they would stay for no longer than two months so as not to wear out their welcome, and then they would move on. There would be some resentment when one of the family members said they couldn't take the two of them and another sibling had to house them for a while. I could tell from the way my father talked about it that he didn't ever want to be in that position.

I remember once I thought it would be funny to run around the dining room table, pick up the silverware, and hide it before dad and the part-time employees came in for lunch. When my mom saw that the silverware was missing, she broke down in tears of exhaustion. I felt awful and quickly let her in on my prank. It made an impression on me, because she seemed pretty cheerful most of the time. Being a kid, I didn't stop to think how hard her life was being a farmer's wife.

I knew my dad was stressed out. He would often take out his anger at the animals, shouting at them or shooing them too aggressively. I was a sensitive kid and I hated watching him treat them that way. I also got very upset whenever a sick animal had to be euthanized. I couldn't stand to see them die—even if they were just chickens or turkeys.

Rusty, who was two-and-a-half years older than I was, couldn't help noticing my sensitivity. I could cry easily if my feelings were hurt or when

I was sad for the animals. Rusty was a lot tougher and decided it would be amusing to taunt me to tears regularly. I remember getting very frustrated and angry at him, but I couldn't control my feelings. My mom would soothe me, and Rusty would apologize and promise not to do it again—but then, of course, he would. I think he was more my father's son while I was my mother's. He seemed to take on some of dad's anger and express it toward me. It was kid's stuff, but it really bothered me because I was exquisitely sensitive.

To some degree, I was able to get back at Rusty in the mornings. I was an early riser with high energy. He liked to sleep in, so I made sure to try to wake him up early. I would also annoy him when he wanted to just sit and read a book. "Cut it out, Bambino!" he'd say, but to no avail.

Our farm was miles from the school or anyone else's house, so I didn't have a choice of playmates. Scotty, Lawrence's son, was a little younger than I was and would show up sometimes to see if I wanted to play with him. I was always climbing over a fence and running through the woods or picking my way across the rocks by the stream. Because Scotty was so young and little, he'd fall behind, lose track of me, and wander off to find something else to do. I never found him to be very much fun. Occasionally, I'd agree to play farmer with him. He'd be my dad and I'd be his. But I'd get bored with that and soon I'd be running off to the woods or stream, leaving Scotty behind.

I also tried to enjoy playing with Jeff, a boy about my age whose father was a friend of my mom's and who lived down the road at his family's farm, but he was quiet and introspective so we had little in common. His brother Wayne was a year older than Rusty, and I would have liked to hang out with the two of them, but Rusty wasn't having it. Consequently, I ended up playing mostly by myself or with our collies. I spent a lot of time outdoors and loved that. My father built a two-acre pond and I had a little rowboat. I'd wake up at 5:30 a.m. and head down there just as the morning fog was rolling off the surface of the water. I'd put the dogs in the boat and start rowing. After a while, I'd stop and just look at the beauty around me. As I sat there, sometimes I'd think it would be nice to have a companion to share this wonder.

Some mornings, I would wake up in the morning and sit downstairs and turn the TV on. At six a.m., "The Star-Spangled Banner" came on because there wasn't any programming overnight. Then, they would broadcast what was called the "Sunrise Movie," an old black-and-white film from the fifties, forties, or thirties that would run until 7:30 a.m. I liked to watch the Roy Rogers westerns and the gangster movies with James Cagney, Humphrey Bogart, or Edward G. Robinson. I remember thinking I'd like to grow up to be like Dean Martin, a tough soldier with a cigarette hanging from his mouth, getting into bar fights and decking some guy before getting the pretty girl in the end. One day, I watched *The Incredible Shrinking Man,* a sci-fi flick about a fellow who for some reason starts to shrink and ends up in his daughter's dollhouse fighting off his own cat, who is clawing at him. Then, he has to attack a spider with a pin that's bigger than he is, and finally he shrinks down so small that he disappears into the screen, never to be seen again. How small can you be and still be alive? I thought the whole idea was fascinating but incredibly scary.

I liked to climb the big maple tree in our front yard. Once in a while, I would get stuck up there and call for my mother. She would come running out to catch me because in trying to get down from the tree, I would often slip and fall. One day, when I was about five years old, she came running out to catch me and didn't show up in time. I fell and bit my lip and had to go to the local family doctor, Dr. Bush, who didn't believe in applying Lidocaine for pain because he felt it increased the risk of infection. He sewed up my lip with three sutures without anything to numb the area. You might think I would be scared or cry, but it seemed like an exciting adventure to me.

We had an old dog, Cindy, who liked to sit next to the pantry behind the house. She was old and arthritic and would fall asleep there, which meant that to get into the pantry, my mother would have to push her gently with her foot in order to wake her up and get her to move. Early one morning, I tried the same thing because I wanted to open the pantry door, but I guess my push wasn't so gentle. She woke up suddenly and snapped at my leg. I still have the scar on my ankle where the canine teeth punctured both sides of my leg. That didn't feel like much of an adventure, and I steered clear of Cindy after that.

I had to get a few stitches once after slipping off the bean picker, but for the most part, my little scrapes didn't scare or upset me. I was proud to show off my stitches! The only thing I was afraid of was a ghost or monster hiding in the closet or under my bed. It was a 200-year old farmhouse, originally a log cabin, and years later, I learned my great-grandfather had died in my room. Who knows what spirits lingered there? Maybe I was sensitive to them. Or, maybe I was just a typical kid imagining something scary in the dark places of our house.

I wasn't completely isolated living on the farm, though. There were some social outlets—the local Cub Scout pack, for instance. What I remember most about that was picking on a heavyset kid named Eddie who stuck out as being different. In retrospect, I probably bullied him because I was angry about being mistreated by my brother. Unlike Rusty, Eddie didn't talk back or take a swing at me. He was gentle and kind of slow, so he was an easy target. No one stopped me and I didn't have the self-awareness to know why I was calling him names or poking him. It wasn't like today. Adults wouldn't intervene or even notice and the kids just accepted that this was the way things were.

Fortunately for Eddie, I ended up dropping Cub Scouts when my mom tired of being a den mother. Instead, I got involved in 4-H—a club for farm kids. I had my own little project raising turkeys. Every morning, I'd wake up and go out to water them and feed them. I took care of them from the day they were born until they were six months old and ready for slaughter. My dad took over that part. Rusty had his own turkeys he was raising for 4-H, too, so I was on my own watering and feeding all my birds. I must have been ten or eleven, and already I had a strong work ethic. When the turkeys went to market, I made $250, which is about the equivalent of $2500 in today's dollars. It was quite a haul! My parents told me to save all the money for college, so I did.

When I wasn't tending to my turkeys, I would play or follow my father around until he'd get angry at the animals and I'd want to hide. I had a sense that I should keep my head low, and stay below the radar screen. I didn't want to be in his way when he was fuming! I never talked to him or my mom, or Rusty, or anyone about that. They seemed to take his irritability in stride. I got the message that I shouldn't be upset. I figured I must just be too sensitive. I didn't talk about my feelings or expect other people to ask whether I was upset.

As I got older, I stopped crying when my brother teased me and learned to stand up to him. By middle school, I was about his height, which gave me a lot more courage when it came to Rusty and his mocking ways. I had overcome the bedwetting that he tormented me about. "I'll tell the other kids about you if you don't do what I say!" he'd warn. My mother and father didn't give me a hard time about the fact that I was wetting the bed far past the age of two, but Rusty saw it as tool for negotiation. That ended when I finally developed the ability to stay dry through the night— or awaken from my deep slumber to use the bathroom. I always played hard and slept hard, so I just didn't get the internal signal to wake up.

One day, when he was in ninth grade and I was in seventh, Rusty and I were waiting for the school bus. My father had bought us go-karts to get around the farm, so for several years, we'd ride them a half mile down the tar-and-chip road to the bus stop and stash them behind a hill. Then we'd peer down the road to see if the bus was coming. By this time, we were both adolescents—in fact, I was almost as big as Rusty was—and dad let us drive his 1956 blue paneled Chevrolet truck to the bus stop. For whatever reason, Rusty and I started getting into it and shoving each other in the truck. We saw the bus come up the road and got out to meet it, but as Rusty got on in front of me, I was still mad, so I kicked him in the butt from behind, making him stumble. Rusty jumped off the bus and swung his book bag at me. Melvin, the usual driver of bus 53, was having none of this and drove off. When I realized I was going to miss our ride, I took off after the bus at top speed yelling and waving at him. No luck. I walked back toward Rusty. By this time, we realized that missing the bus was more important than carrying on our fight. If we missed school, we would both be in big trouble with dad.

Just then, we saw the car that belonged to our neighbor Ronnie coming up the road. Quickly, Rusty and I stuck our thumbs out to hitch hike. Ronnie picked us up and we breathed a sigh of relief. After school, Rusty practiced with the track team as usual and I took the bus home right when class let out. Dad spotted me as soon as I got to the farmhouse and said he needed to talk to me.

"You see that razor strap on the wall?" he said before I even got my coat off. "I got a call from the bus driver apologizing for having to leave you boys. When Rusty gets home, the two of you are going to learn a lesson about fighting. My father only had to use that strap on me one time for me to get the message!"

I froze. I had really messed up this time. He had never taken that antique strap off the wall.

"Now, come and help me inseminate the turkeys!" he said, and stomped out.

Sheepishly, I followed him to one of the buildings where we did this little procedure. I'd hold the female turkey down while he would artificially inseminate her using a little pistol-like device with a tube. I worked with him for an hour and a half, and the whole time I was extra cooperative and friendly, chatting away with my dad until Rusty got home. By that point, dad's mood had shifted and we heard nothing more about the brawl at the bus stop. Those turkeys saved us!

After that, Rusty realized I was too big to pick on anymore, and if I'd saved him a licking, maybe it wasn't so bad to have me around. That was our last, and only, real fight.

My dad never actually used the strap on us, though he threatened to. I was a cooperative kid so I didn't get into much trouble. There is one memory, however, that really sticks with me, which I've reflected on a lot in my recovery. One pretty spring morning, when I was about four years old, our family was just about to leave for church. I was in my only nice set of clothes when I accidentally stepped, hard, in a puddle that had formed in the broken concrete of our walkway after the rain the night before. The splash was big enough not just to get my clothes dirty but my dad's suit as well. He grabbed me and spanked me forcefully. I was so scared I wet my pants. When he realized that, he growled, "You're such a big baby. Maybe we should let him go to church and let everyone see what a baby he is. You wet the bed almost every night. You're too old for that!"

Even then, I knew his anger wasn't justified. But I had no idea what to do about my own feelings of shame and humiliation. A four-year-old can't consciously process what's just happened and consciously choose not to let it bother him. The incident taught me that I ought to tread carefully around my dad when he was upset. It would be many years before I could look back at this and understand how damaging that was for me given that I was so young. I would have to learn to let go of the need to please people and stay clear of their anger or disappointment, to not take on their emotions.

Even though there were moments when my father's mood was intimidating, more often I was happy and enjoying life on the farm. There's a lot about that experience I wish my kids could have, but it's not possible given that I'm a surgeon and we live in the suburbs near my work. I'm glad that I can look back now and see the origins of some of my issues, and recognize the parallels to my father's life. I'm glad he was able to see at a certain point that life is too short to go for the money and be in chronic stress. I'm glad my mom and dad had a good marriage that gave us emotional stability in our home. And I'm glad that for all our competitiveness, Rusty and I still have a good relationship. It was a happy childhood, and it prepared me to have the discipline and perseverance to follow my dream of becoming a surgeon that began to take form when I was still in grade school.

A Glimmer
of an Idea

Chapter Five

U ntil I went to kindergarten, the longest amount of time I had
been separated from my mom was an hour or so during Sunday
school. Kindergarten was only for a half day back in that era,
so my mom would only be inaccessible for a few hours, but that was a big
deal to me because she had always been available whenever I needed her.
Once she walked me into the classroom, I looked for someone I knew,
but every child was unfamiliar to me. I did *not* want to be there! Then,
I spotted something I had never seen before: Two little girls who looked
exactly alike. "They're identical twins," my new teacher explained. I didn't
know what that was, but I was mesmerized by the two of them mirroring
each other as they rode tricycles in a circle. I guess the novelty of it was
enough to distract me from my mother slipping out of the room. I found
out that I was allowed to ride the tricycles too, so after a day or two, I
decided kindergarten wasn't so bad after all.

When the day came for me to do Show and Tell for the first time, I
knew just what I wanted to bring in. In our home, we had several scientific

books and one in particular intrigued me. It showed forty stages of embryological development, from the sperm joining an egg to the division into two cells, four, eight, then sixteen, all the way up until the fortieth picture, which was of a baby. I remember thinking, *This is a miracle. How cool is this?*

My mother didn't think I should bring in that particular book but didn't explain why, so I decided to go ahead and bring it anyway. I was very excited to show it to my kindergarten teacher. She said, "Oh, wow. That's really nice, Steve. But I think this is a book for home, not for school." I was disappointed. How could she not be interested and want the class to see what I was seeing? I did show it to one of the other students, too, and he was as unimpressed as she was. I didn't get how he and the teacher reacted. This was incredible stuff! Why weren't they amazed, like I was? *If only I could be a girl!* I thought. *Then I could become pregnant and give birth to a baby.* Unfair!

I guess I had a sense of wonderment of the universe at an early age.

I got along well with the girls—I even had a little girlfriend in first grade. The boys didn't seem quite as interesting to me until I got older and I discovered sports. Girls rarely played sports back then so if I wanted to participate in sports, I was going to have to spend more time with boys.

Both my brother and I played baseball in the summer starting with Pee Wee League and then, later, graduating into Little League. I enjoyed the camaraderie of baseball and got along with all the kids. I was a good player and had fun, but I always felt a little different, a little separated. That's a common theme for alcoholics and addicts actually: not really feeling they fit in. It wasn't necessarily a reality. The other boys were accepting of me. But I was hesitant around them, afraid I might not be good enough for them, or that I might do or say something wrong and be rejected. My sensitivity probably had a big influence on my perception.

To protect myself from potentially being ostracized, I became a perfectionist. If I felt I couldn't do well at something, I wouldn't even try. I worked very hard at anything I thought I could be good at, including sports.

Years later in rehab, I took a personality profile test and it showed I had a hint of narcissism. Hmmm, that wasn't something I wanted to discover about myself! But the psychologist explained that a person can become very self-focused if his basic needs for an immediate, nurturing response aren't met in the first year of life. The child develops a sense that he has to do extra to get attention and love. I'm sure that like most babies in the postwar era, I logged a lot of time alone in a playpen. Succeeding in sports was one way to make my parents notice me and earn the approval of the other kids. My father would have loved to see me play, he told me later, but couldn't come to many of my games when he was a turkey farmer because he was so busy. Still, he came to the important ones, and that helped me believe that I was onto something: hard work leads to success which leads to love and approval. And as my brother and I got older and my dad didn't have to spend as much time taking care of the chickens as he had the turkeys, dad started showing up at all our games. Later, when Rusty and I played high school football, dad even bought a handheld movie camera to film us. He was very proud of our abilities on the field.

In addition to playing baseball as a kid, and getting pretty good at it, I swam. By kindergarten, I knew how to do the crawl. I had no fear of the water, even though I was very young. Ellen, one of my cousins, taught swimming lessons at the Manchester Lion's Club swimming pool. My mother told the club owners that they had to let Ellen teach me as well as my brother—a package deal, so to speak. I got even better at swimming, although my brother wasn't very happy that once again, I was tagging along behind him. I always liked hanging out with my brother's friends better than my own, and Rusty probably wanted to have some privacy with them rather than have me there like an eager puppy trying to be a part of whatever they were doing.

In elementary school, I joined up with a kid named Mike Palmer and three or four other boys in walking around trying to intimidate the other boys. We called ourselves the Freedom Fighters and would march around with locked arms chanting, "We are the freedom fighters." I was more of a follower, and I guess I thought I was being tough like my father and his

World War II buddies. There were only about 50 kids in the school but we found enough boys to pick on to keep us feeling tough.

For the most part, though, I felt I got along with everybody. The girls seemed to like me despite the rough and tumble types I was hanging around with, and I always had a girlfriend who thought I was something special.

Meanwhile, I looked forward to the day when I could outshine my brother in sports. I didn't outshine him in academics; both of us were average students at best. My reading ability, study skills, and test scores didn't match up with how smart I actually was. I had an easy time understanding the material, but proving that was difficult for me. I wasn't sure why. It also didn't help that I talked a lot in class; the "conduct" section of my report card was always sprinkled with checkmarks. One day, when a group of kids was called to the office for talking in class the day before, I was called too. I'd been absent that day, but they were rounding up the usual suspects and that clearly included me—whether I was actually at school that day or not!

My Aunt Jean, who taught at my school, still laughs with me about that. I do have to credit her with telling my mom that regardless of my grades, I was a smart kid. My mother believed in me—and Rusty. Every day, she sat us down at the kitchen table and made sure we did our homework.

In sixth grade, everyone in the class took a standardized test and when the results came back, the teacher told everyone that there was a student who did better than everyone else, which was a surprise to her because this particular student did not get good marks. I thought, *That's interesting. I wonder who it is?* When I got my test score back and saw the number, I knew it was me. It was a revelation. I was smarter than I thought I was! But why did I struggle so much? It was frustrating for me.

Many years later, one of my sons would be tested for ADHD. As the evaluators explained the criteria and symptoms, I thought, *Wait a minute. This describes me!* High energy, difficulty sitting still, smart but prone to being an underachiever—that was definitely me as a kid.

It was when I was nine that I had the second childhood experience that would solidify for me what I wanted to do when I grew up. I was already fascinated by science and the human body. That year, my grandfather had some prostate problems and for whatever reason, I was there at the urologist's office with him. I was trying to read a little yellow hardcover book called *Ribsy*, a book about the adventures of a dog who escapes from his family's car and does a lot of wandering around and getting into trouble before finding his way back home. I was trying to focus on the words but feeling antsy. I started to look around the waiting room and reception area and count all of the people around me. My grandfather came out of the consultation room and the receptionist lady asked him for ten dollars. He reached in his wallet, pulled out a ten dollar bill, and gave it to her. In that moment, an insight came to me. I turned to my mother and said, "Wow! He just gave that lady ten dollars. Is everybody in this office who is seeing the doctor going to have to pay ten dollars, too?" She said yes. "So you mean he's going to make a hundred dollars today?" She said yes. And I said, "Oh, I want to be a doctor then!"

I didn't know how many books I was going to have to read in order to be able to collect those types of fees, but I knew I wanted to be a doctor!

Then, when I was about 12, I was riding in the car with my mother one day when I had a strange experience that I couldn't understand at the time. We were driving on Houcksville Road and had just passed the house where my great uncle Tom lived and were coming up on a house where another of my mother's relatives lived. I sensed a shift in the energy, and it drove me into a state of contemplation. The Chinese say there are places on earth where the chi, or life force energy, is especially strong. I believe that was one of those places—an energy vortex. There was nothing special about that day or what we were doing, and yet I suddenly found myself wondering, "What am I here for? Why am I on the earth? What's the purpose of my life?" I had never asked myself questions like this before, and I think they came up in that moment because I was picking up on that powerful chi.

I waited in a state of openness for the answers to come to me. Then, I had an inner knowing that I was to be of service to other people. I wondered, "What does that look like? How am I going to help others?" And somehow, three ideas popped into my head at once. I could be a minister. I could be politician. Or I could be a doctor.

Although I had been sure I wanted to be a doctor, I felt the need to think about all the possibilities that had just come to me in an almost mystical way. I thought about politicians. Hmmm … Didn't most of them lie? I was an honest kid, so being a politician wasn't resonating for me. Then, I turned my mind to ministers. They all seemed to be somewhat poor, and seeing how worries about money had affected my parents who had lived through the Depression, I didn't want to not have enough money. Besides, I wasn't sure how much impact ministers had on the lives of others. Doctors, I knew, made good money, and obviously, they helped other people.

I looked out the window at the cirrus clouds in the pale blue sky. My mind was made up. Being a healer would be my life path.

Chapter Six

Buckling Down

M iddle school was a time of big changes for me: My truce with Rusty and my newfound interest in girls were the two biggest ones. I was still spending a lot of time with the local boys because I was into sports, but now I realized I wanted to spend more time around the girls I knew. The girls liked to talk about big ideas, which I enjoyed. In fact, later on, in high school, a girl nicknamed me "the Philosopher" and it stuck. In junior high, I always seemed to have a girlfriend to put my arm around and a group of girls who would hang around with me and my friends.

The pond where I had spent mornings when I was younger wishing for friends to join me became a place for everyone to get together. We had ice skating parties in the winter when it froze over. In the summer, we would swim out to the raft made out of wooden planks and four 40-gallon barrels. The girls didn't mind that the guys pushed them into the water or capsized the big tire inner tubes they floated on. It was simple fun and we all laughed a lot. The universe had finally answered my longing to share that beautiful, natural spot with other kids.

Meanwhile, at school I wasn't exactly a star student. I was getting Cs and Ds, but it didn't keep me off of athletic teams like it would if I were a student today. And as long as I was learning something, making an effort, and not flunking out, my parents didn't give me grief. My brother struggled in school, too, and everything my parents had tried to get him to do better hadn't improved the situation. With him setting the bar, they couldn't make a big deal about my grades. Besides, I was helping out on the farm, so I was responsible. As far as I was concerned, how to succeed academically was a mystery but not one I felt compelled to figure out. All that changed when I was in eighth grade after my family went on a ski vacation and I became friends with a kid named Keith.

Now, the first time I had skied was at the hunting lodge of a friend of my father's. It was in the Wisp ski area in Oakland, Maryland, about eight miles away from the slope. This fellow had a string of trailers that lay dormant after hunting season was over, and it dawned on him that he might make a little money renting them out to skiers.

I always loved snow. I used to sit by the window and watch each snowflake come down, and I had a pair of wooden skis I played around with in the snow in our backyard. The first time I was able to ski on an actual ski hill, I thought it was the greatest thing ever. I fell over again and again, but I didn't care. By the third day, I was way past skiing the bunny hill and was on the black diamond trail, zipping around and keeping up with the lodge owner's kids who had been skiing for six or seven years. Sometimes I found the patience to wait in line for the two-man chair lift or the old-style Poma lift, which consisted of a disk with a spring-loaded shaft that attaches to an overhead cable that pulls you up the hill. Mostly, though, I got myself into the much shorter line for the tow rope. My vinyl-covered mittens got eaten up by the rope that was in a constant state of motion, pulling skiers up the mountainside as they held on to it. I quickly learned to let it slide through my mittens, tearing them up gradually, before clamping on. If I didn't, I'd be yanked forward and fall into the snow. It was all great fun to me. So when I overheard my classmate

Keith tell one of our eight grade teachers he would be gone for a week skiing in Vermont, I immediately started asking him about his trip.

The next thing I knew, my family was going to Stowe, Vermont, with Keith's. Stowe is one of those quaint little New England towns with a pretty white church whose tall steeple reaches into the sky, and a big fountain downtown that froze into a beautiful ice sculpture in winter. The Von Trapp family had a ski lodge there for cross-country skiers, and Keith told me some of the downhill ski hills actually lent skiers ponchos fashioned from wool blankets to keep them warm while waiting for the ski lifts. We relied on nylon parkas, plus plenty of tea, hot chocolate, and coffee to warm us up when we got back into the lodge.

When I returned to school, I noticed Keith's name on the student honor roll, which was posted on the wall near the front office. It had been great competing with Keith on the ski hill, but now that I saw he was able to make the honor roll, I wanted to compete with him academically. His father was an engineer, which I knew meant he was a college graduate. I wanted what Keith had: success in school and the possibility of going to college like his dad had done.

"It's easy to get As and Bs," he told me. I wanted to believe him, so I decided to work hard and see if I could do better in school.

Soon afterward, while I was still in ninth grade, some premed students came in to talk to students who were college bound. I'd made no secret of my dream of becoming a doctor, so the teachers told me I should take a few minutes out to meet our visitors. They told me it was important to get good grades, and silently, I committed to doing even better in that department.

As it turned out, my girlfriend at the time really helped me—but not by teaching me study habits or going over notes with me. This girl was very cute and sweet, but she would call me on the phone and talk on and on about who said what and what so-and-so was doing. Before long, I was tuning out. To get her off the phone without hurting her feelings, I would tell her that I had to go do my homework. After I hung up, I felt guilty if I didn't actually open my books, so before you know it, my little white lie to her turned into my actually spending more time studying. I started getting better grades and realized, "Hey, I can do this. I can be a B student, at least, and maybe even an A student."

Around this time, we had a drug education unit in school. It was the late sixties and parents were afraid of what their kids might be getting into. The basic approach was to scare the hell out of us. The adults had probably seen news footage of drugged-out hippies and wanted to be absolutely certain their kids went nowhere near those long-haired pot smokers. They taught us about the horrible things that happened to addicts and implied that if you used drugs, even marijuana, it would lead to disaster. I remember one cautionary tale about a man who took LSD, hallucinated, and ended up jumping off a building to his death because he thought he could fly. The teachers told us that marijuana was a gateway drug that would lead you to using the harder stuff and ruining your life.

I have to admit the message worked when we were that age, but not later as we got into high school and college. We overcame our fear and gave into our curiosity about pot, only to discover the adults had lied to us about how it would turn us into crazed drug fiends overnight. In fact, it just gave us the munchies and made us silly or, in my case, mellow and introspective. I remember smoking pot during my senior year of high school and staring at one of those posters designed to be viewed in black light—illuminated by an ultraviolet lamp. This particular poster had little rocks and flowers hidden under rocks, and even little bugs on the rocks and flowers, none of which you could see if you were straight but you'd notice them if you were high. It was psychedelic.

Even so, I was very clean cut. When one of the kids at school who was known as a stoner asked me if I had some pot to sell, I got scared. How did he know to ask me? I hurriedly denied that I touched the stuff, and he looked at me skeptically. I didn't have to be high to be paranoid. I sure didn't want anyone finding out that I enjoyed a little pot here and there. I liked the reputation I had as a responsible kid who was starting to do better in school.

The way my friends and I saw it, if our parents and the adults in the community had lied to us about how dangerous pot was, they must have lied to us about drugs in general. They had tried to scare us about cigarettes, too, but we'd survived a few puffs behind a barn or the school without getting addicted to smoking. We started to assess our risk according to what other people we knew were trying, and what their experiences were—exactly what the adults hoped we wouldn't do. I didn't try anything harder than pot in high school, but the sense that we had been oversold on the danger of drugs stuck with me.

While drugs that were unfamiliar to our parents were scaring them, they weren't as frightened about teenagers using alcohol. Because of the Vietnam draft, the laws had been changed around the country so drinking at eighteen was legal, which meant some high schoolers could legally purchase alcohol. Adults didn't want younger teenagers drinking, but they assumed their kids would grow up to drink socially just as they had. It wasn't very difficult to get liquor or beer when you were fifteen or sixteen. Teenagers would have keg parties in their families' barns and the parents were okay with it as long as we arranged for someone sober to pick us up. Their attitude was, "We'd rather know where you're drinking."

I'd gotten drunk on beer one night the summer before ninth grade and ended up with an awful hangover that turned me off of alcohol for a while. But a couple years later, I decided to try it again. My friends and I got a hold of some Mr. Boston Cherry Vodka—the sort of liquor that adults use sparingly in cocktails but teens want to drink straight because it's so sweet it disguises the flavor of the alcohol. I had quite a buzz going by the time our group headed off to a local carnival. There, I ran into Mike, one of the tough kids I'd been in the Freedom Fighters with. In my half-drunken state, I took offense at something he said. I might have been overly sensitive and paranoid, or I might have picked up on some condescension there. But whatever it was, I was mad. I had a milkshake in my hand and tossed it in his face as I shouted at him. I managed to get out of there without him beating me up—I guess all that running practice in sports served me well. Afterward, I was scared, not of him so much as scared of alcohol. I had lost control. That had never happened before. It would be a long time before I drank again.

By tenth grade, I was definitely doing better in school. I was also playing a lot of sports: baseball, football, basketball, and track. I was skiing whenever I could, too. In my junior year, I got interested in lacrosse, which I had seen played in the athletic fields of private schools but which hadn't yet come to my high school. I talked one of my teachers into starting a lacrosse club so I could have a chance to play with a team instead of simply against the wall of my family's barn. On an athletic field, I was an intense competitor. I got my anger and aggression out through sports.

When I was in tenth grade, I competed with Rusty for the defensive cornerback position on the varsity football team, which he'd been the year before—and I was chosen. I had finally bested him in sports. He doesn't remember this being the case but I do! His story was that he chose to play offense rather than defense. Whatever the real story was, that football experience was a big turning point for me. My relationship with him, which had been getting better ever since our fistfight, changed from adversarial to friendly after that. Then again, I believe the universe responds to what type of energy you're generating. Once I felt he and I were equal, he seemed to treat me better. I had changed the dynamic by changing myself.

I was becoming more and more self-motivated. I realized if I just did my homework, I could get As and Bs and get my name onto the honor roll alongside Keith's. My junior year, I actually earned straight As for the first time. As senior year came closer, I was determined to keep up the momentum.

Chapter Seven   # Work Hard

C oach O'Connell, from the football team at Washington and Lee University in Virginia, was in my high school recruiting. I was told he wanted to meet with me because I was the captain of the football team. He also wanted to meet with my friend Rick, who was co-captain.

I'd wanted to go to a small, private college, and the ones I had visited had responded to my question about playing football with, "Oh, sure, you can try out for the team if you like." They weren't exactly courting me. But here was a coach actually seeking out football players. I hadn't heard of Washington and Lee, and I hoped my grades would impress the coach, even though my rural high school wasn't academically rigorous.

When Rick and I sat down, Coach O'Connell explained to us that Washington and Lee, a private all-male college, was sound academically and had a very good premed program. He said he was looking for smart football players because, well, he couldn't get football players who weren't very smart to go to college. The coach's pitch worked well enough to convince Rick and me to visit the campus and apply. He implied strongly that being a football player would give me the edge with the admissions committee.

At the end of the season of my last year of high school my coach told me I'd been selected as the scholar-athlete to represent the school at the Maryland Football Foundation Hall of Fame. I got to go to a big awards dinner where I was honored, and where I met the football coaches at Washington and Lee University in Maryland again. I did my best to make a good impression at this second meeting with them. It wouldn't be the last time I would try to make a personal connection and get my face out there to improve my chances of getting into a school. In the meantime, I basked in my glory. Athlete and scholar—I liked that!

At last, I got the news, I had been accepted and Rick had, too. I was incredibly excited. My guidance counselor had told me that I might not be premed material, which had really made me mad. He asked me whether I'd considered other options, and I answered bluntly, "No." I understood that my SAT scores weren't the greatest. I tended to choke up on tests, and I knew that was something that might trip me up. But I had an excellent grade point average, I was disciplined and determined, and I was determined to prove him wrong. And I had!

Soon I would learn I wasn't prepared for how demanding a private university premed program would be.

I donned my khaki pants, white shirt, and tie, and moved into the dorms at Washington and Lee, an all-male college that employed and matriculated many a southern gentleman. And then, I cracked the books. But several weeks into my freshman football season at college, I realized I had a problem. The athletics were very time consuming as well as energy consuming. Sleeping with your head on your chemistry book does not result in any intellectual expansion. I was not filling my brain with knowledge through osmosis.

I was taking Calculus, Chemistry, Psychology, and a remedial writing course, and barely getting by in all of them. It seemed I was going to have to drop football to focus on my studies, but the coach gave me a guilt trip about quitting the team in the middle of a weak season. I was hardly their star player or captain, but he made me feel I had no choice but to remain on the team and keep struggling academically. I didn't want to disappoint him or the team. I was what you would call a people pleaser. I decided I would just have to do my best.

My best, however, could be summed up as mediocre. At the end of the semester, I had a 1.7 average. Ouch. At that rate, med school admission was looking unlikely. Worse, I was in danger of not graduating at all. I looked around me at classmates who had come from private schools and thought, *Do I really fit here?* I had long hair, and outside of class, I preferred well-worn jeans to crisp trousers. Besides that, I came from a school where only 28 percent of my graduating class went on to a higher education— and that's only if you count community college, tech school, and beauty school. My summer job before college had been working on an assembly line at a Black & Decker manufacturing plant in Hampstead, Maryland, where I grew up. It was so boring I knew I didn't want to have to end up in a job like that. I wanted to do well, and play sports, too, because I love competing. I wasn't willing to give up my dream of being a doctor. But I had to do something fast if I wanted to keep pace with my classmates.

How could I improve my study skills? I had to employ guesswork. I tried rewriting my lecture notes not once but twice, and that made a difference in what I retained. I began reading every book or handout twice. I learned to get by on five or six hours of sleep. Finally, football season ended and I had more energy. My test scores started improving. It looked as if I was going to make it after all. I would just have to make up for my lousy grades in the semesters to come.

Socially, I was doing pretty well. Both my roommate and I had girlfriends back home, so on weekends, we'd leave campus. I lived four hours from the university, so I spent a lot of time driving. I had gotten to know a few people at college and gone to a few parties, but I didn't feel very connected to campus life given how much time I was spending with my girlfriend, driving, or studying.

I was drinking a little beer to be social despite my concerns about how well I could hold my liquor. Beer was an effective social lubricant for me, and I felt I needed one. One weekend while I was on a campout in a friend's big backyard, I got into a shouting match with a guy my age. He'd gotten it into his head that I had been coming on to his girlfriend. She had flirted with me, I suppose, but I hadn't really made much of it. And I didn't know she had a boyfriend. I found out when he came up to me as a group of us were walking on top of a hill on my friend's land. "I'll kick your ass!" he shouted. Then he went into a string of insults and threats.

At first, I was bewildered and a little disoriented. It didn't help that I'd had two or three beers, so mentally processing his string of crazy, angry accusations was taking a little longer than usual. Then, I pulled it together to form a fist and take a swing at him just before he was going to take one at me. I lost my balance and fell on my face in the dirt, and started rolling down the hill we were standing on. I jumped up quickly, but embarrassment rushed through me.

Fortunately, my friend Rick, who was a pretty tough guy and at 6' 3", not someone the other guy had any desire to mess with, jumped in and broke up the fight. I was humiliated but tried to tell myself that no one would remember my pathetic attempt to defend myself. I hated that I had once again lost control because of drinking. I decided I'd have to be careful when it came to alcohol—even if I was just drinking beer.

At Washington and Lee, they had a second football season in the spring, and I really wanted to take the risk and play. It was only for a few weeks. Unfortunately, at the same time, I had a six-week, intensive class in quantitative chemistry. I got the best grade on the first exam out of anyone, but two weeks later, after a few football practices and a game, I took another exam in the class and scored the lowest grade. There was no denying that football, and not my study habits, was going to be the end of my med school dream if I didn't quit the team. I just couldn't risk blowing college. I didn't want to meet with the coach and take on his disappointment and find myself caving in again just to get out of feeling guilty, so I sent him a letter telling him of my decision. He accepted my resignation without calling me in to lay another guilt trip on me, which was a big relief.

At my college, it was typical for students to spend the first year in the dorms, join a fraternity, and move into a house with their frat brothers their sophomore year. Since I'd spent my weekends commuting back home to see my girlfriend, I had missed out on the fraternity scene. I didn't want to go back to the dorms. I ended up moving into a four-bedroom house off campus with some fellow students I didn't know very well who, like me, had not become part of fraternity life. Rick had left school, gotten married, and transferred to another college, so he was out of my life. I liked him, but it bothered me that he regularly got very drunk. In retrospect, I think he had a drinking problem. At the time, I didn't understand why he couldn't just drink a few beers and not get totally out of control. That didn't happen to me—well, of course, that wasn't true, but I wasn't ready to admit that. My reasoning was, if I had learned how to drink without getting drunk, why couldn't he?

I got a new girlfriend, Annie, who attended Roanoke College an hour south of Washington and Lee, so that cut down on my driving time and gave me a built-in social life, as she had plenty of friends. The two of us would talk about big ideas and what we were studying. She was a good influence on me, and I was getting good grades. I later realized she came from a family of alcoholics, which would explain why she didn't break up with me after a particularly ugly incident. I had been drinking and got angry with her—I don't remember what it was about, but I slapped her. The slap was so out of character for me that we both stood there for a moment, stunned at what happened. I apologized to her over and over, and she forgave me and told me she understood. To her, that behavior wasn't abnormal. I took a cue from her, so while I was ashamed, here I had someone validating what I desperately wanted to believe: that it was no big deal. Only in recovery, years later, did I think back to that day. I wondered if Annie had gone on to realize that being drunk is never an excuse for a man to hit a woman. It was a horrible memory I tried to block out of my mind.

That year, when I went home on winter break, a friend decided it would be fun to drink a shot of beer a minute for 60 minutes. I don't remember where we got that stupid idea. We would have passed out long before we even got to 15 minutes. The two of us did a few shots with liquor from my parents' liquor cabinet and got drunk enough to come up with another stupid idea: to drive to a small town nearby where there was a Jack-in-the-Box to get something to eat. My friend got behind the wheel, and we managed to get there without driving off the road and hitting something. We got our food and walked into the parking lot, where there was a black guy around our age laughing at something. I didn't have a lot of experience with black people, which was typical in a farming community, but it's not as if I thought of myself as prejudiced. I had black friends at college who were on the football team. If I was racist, I wasn't aware of it.

Because I was completely smashed, I got into that paranoid frame of mind I'd experienced at the carnival years before when I'd been drinking. I became convinced this guy was laughing at me. Out of nowhere, I started shouting racial slurs at him. My friend was stunned and so was the stranger. The fellow sized me up; starting yelling back—and then he punched me in the mouth. Well, I deserved it.

I ended up losing a tooth, but at least I didn't get arrested. When I sobered up back home, I was embarrassed and a little scared. I had actually caused permanent damage to my body by getting drunk and out of control. I had a good dentist, who capped the tooth, but even today, I can see the subtle difference in how that tooth looks. It's a reminder of that awful day. Where did all that anger and ugliness come from? That wasn't me … Was it?

The incident was really unsettling. I thought about the little experiment of doing shots, my experience at the carnival a few years back, and the campout, and decided beer was okay, but the hard stuff—especially the dark stuff—was off limits. I felt a little better after setting that boundary with myself. It had been humiliating to have to tell my parents how I lost my tooth. I was never going to let anything like that happen again.

Famous last words!!

Chapter Eight   # Play Hard

I continued to do well in school, and in my junior year, I joined a fraternity and moved into an apartment with three other frat brothers who also liked to study hard and play hard. I wasn't smoking pot, but I was getting drunk on beer just about every Friday night. That's right: Despite all these incidents of getting out of control when drinking, I continued. I reasoned that everyone drank to be sociable. The frat house antics in *Animal House* with John Belushi, which came out a few years after I joined a fraternity, weren't that far from what I experienced. It was all good fun, right? I had lots of rationalizations for drinking.

During one party, to be funny and cool, I drove my Yamaha dirt bike up the front steps of the house, across the porch, through the living room, and out the back door. Everyone laughed at how crazy and daring I was. I loved that I had made an impression on everyone.

I was buzzed on Colt 45 malt liquor and kept on drinking it into the night. After the party ended, I drove home with a friend who was riding on the seat behind me. On the gravel road to the Maury River house,

I turned back to say something to him and lost control. We skidded, and he walked away without injury, but I scraped up my shoulder and knee enough to have to quit the lacrosse team. I had sworn off football, but lacrosse was less demanding, and I seemed to be able to do all the studying I needed. And once again—because clearly, it takes hitting me over the head several times for me to get the message—I got a bad grade and realized I was overestimating how well I was doing academically. As for my dirt bike accident, my excuse was that it was fairly new to me and I hadn't mastered the controls. I didn't let myself think about the role alcohol played.

Despite my partying, I never drank two nights in a row. I've always had GERD, or gastro esophageal reflux disease, so my stomach would bother me the next day after a hard night of drinking. That was enough incentive to halt the drinking until the next weekend. I felt I was in control of my behavior. I used typical alcoholic reasoning: Since I only got drunk one night out of the weekend, not two, I didn't have a drinking problem.

One of my best memories of that year was at a backyard party on a warm September evening in 1977. KC and the Sunshine Band was playing as the sun set behind the mountains. The girls in their brightly colorful sundresses were pretty and quick to smile at me and say "yes" when I asked them to dance. I had the perfect gin-and-tonic. I fit in now. The wealthy girls from the nearby colleges laughed at my jokes and flipped their long hair to flirt with me. The guys from private prep schools and prestigious urban public schools saw me as one of them. As I sat there listening to "I'm Your Boogie Man" spinning on the turntable, I felt I had arrived.

But being in the frat house environment, I began to accept the "work hard, play hard" attitude. I felt entitled to cut loose on a weekend, believing I would be able to juggle the work and the play to reach my goal of getting into a good medical school at the end of my four years.

Confidence is a good thing. Unfortunately, it turns out I had a little too much of it. I was wracking up too many Bs and not enough As, so my GPA was 3.3—not good enough for med school. In the late spring of my junior year, I didn't do as well on my MCAT—the Medical College Admissions Test—as I wanted to. It was the old problem of choking up when I was taking a test. It dawned on me that I was probably going to have some trouble getting accepted into medical school. I tried not to worry, and to enjoy experiences like working at Duke University's marine biology lab in Beauford, North Carolina as part of a class. The Outer Banks were breathtaking in their beauty, and I loved the class—and my premed program.

But soon, I realized the worries I'd set aside were justified: None of the medical schools I applied to accepted me.

It was a blow. But I just couldn't give up. I knew I could take the MCATs again and apply once more to the medical schools I was interested in, but my grade point average needed to come up, too. How was I going to make it happen? I remember distinctly walking between the science building and chemistry building one bright spring day before graduation and experiencing what I now know is a nudge from the universe. Dr. James S. Starling, Jr., an older and distinguished professor that I had taken a couple of classes from, called out in his southern drawl, "Hello Mr. Heird! So what are you doing next year? Will you be going to medical school?"

I returned his smile, but in that moment I made a choice to tell him the truth even though it was embarrassing. "No, Dr. Starling. I didn't get into med school. Anywhere."

His face grew serious and his voice became quieter. "Mr. Heird, it is not a crime not to be a doctor."

"But I don't want to be anything but a doctor."

"Well then, Mr. Heird, you will be a doctor."

Hearing that made a real impact on me. He sounded absolute, and I wanted to believe him.

I wasn't going to give up—that much I knew. Instead, I was going to keep my eyes and ears open for other ways to get to where I wanted to go. Meanwhile, I was going to reapply, plan to take the MCATs again, and think about getting some guidance on what to do next. Should I repeat some courses to get a higher grade? That seemed like a possibility.

A few weeks later, on the advice of some of my relatives, I called Dr. Harry Hull, a general surgeon who was retired from the University of

Maryland Hospital, to drop their names and tell him about my plight. "A call from Dr. Hull will get you into med school," I was told. That may have been true once, but it wasn't true anymore. Oh, he was sympathetic, but he explained he really couldn't do anything for me, and that I should definitely retake some courses to increase my GPA. Dr. Hull was nice enough to introduce me to a friend of his named Dr. Willard Allen, who was the chairman of the admissions committee for the school of medicine at U of M. The committee met each year to determine which students were going to be admitted to medical school. Dr. Hull thought maybe getting me in front of the committee chairman would improve my chances of getting on their waiting list. It certainly couldn't hurt.

I met with Dr. Allen and he was very polite and kind to me, but he explained that he couldn't overrule the decisions of the committee or put pressure on them to admit a student who was academically below the other students. He told me I should consider osteopathic school, but I didn't know what that was and didn't feel like looking into it. I was determined to be a Doctor of Medicine, or MD—and preferably, a surgeon, although I would keep my options open.

I decided the best course was to enroll at the University of Maryland College Park as a nondegree graduate student, which meant that I wasn't actually in a graduate program but could take courses that would allow me to raise my 3.3 undergraduate GPA to 3.5—assuming I earned As this time around. I would look much better to Dr. Allen and the medical school admissions committee. Then, I would ace the MCATs somehow. Doing well on tests still stumped me. I had no idea about where I could find help with that. I had to rely on positive thinking.

Before classes began, I moved into an apartment I saw advertised in a local paper by another college student—a stranger—who became my roommate. I was registered for some science courses. I'd like to say my full attention was on earning those As I needed, but as usual, I was distracted by drinking and football season. The school had a great team that year and I loved going to see the games, socializing, and hanging out at a local bar called the Rendezvous, or "the Voo" for short. I was committed to my goal, but I didn't have enough motivation to say no to the beer-at-the-bar-after-the-game scene. Even so, I kept in contact with Dr. Allen to keep my foot in the door and to get his encouragement.

One October day, I went to his office to remind him that I still wanted to get in and ask him if he had any further guidance or ideas for me. Maybe I was going for a pep talk, too. As I sat waiting for my appointment, a woman walked in and sat down next to me, and we struck up a conversation. She said her name was Dr. Satterfield and she was a psychiatrist and Assistant Dean of Student Affairs. She asked what I was up to and I told her my story, to which she said, "If you're really as serious about being a doctor as you say you are, my advice to you would be to go to a foreign medical school. I have eleven students downstairs going through orientation right now who are American but transferred here from foreign medical schools. There are three from Guadalajara, three from the Philippines, one from Italy, one from Spain and one from Belgium—they're from all over, really. You're welcome to come down and meet with them after you meet with Dr. Allen. I'd be glad to introduce you to them and you can get more information about the possibility of going to med school in a foreign country before transferring back here."

"Do you think my chances will be good if I do that?"

"Ever since Congress passed the Kennedy bill to address the doctor shortage," she explained, "all the state schools have a big incentive to keep the class full. By the third year, some med students drop out, so if you want to transfer in from a foreign med, you have a good shot at a spot."

Wow. I hadn't heard about any of this. Did I bump into her out of sheer dumb luck? Or was it the universe once again bringing me an opportunity that resonated with the energy I was sending out? I knew nothing about the Law of Attraction back then, but now I truly believe this is an example of how it works. Your thoughts and desires create a certain vibration that draws you into situations that match up with that vibration.

Before going to meet Dr. Satterfield's students, I met with Dr. Allen as I'd planned and asked him to explain about foreign medical schools. He said, "Of course, there are no guarantees that you will be able to transfer to the University of Maryland School of Medicine after two years of studying medicine abroad"—he had to say that, of course. "But you will have an MD degree and you'll be able to practice medicine in the United States as long as you pass the exams you must take to re-enter the United States medical system."

At that moment, I knew what I was going to do. I went downstairs after that meeting and starting talking to some of the students who had made the same choice I was making—to go to a foreign medical school and then return to the U.S. and earn a U.S. medical degree before going into practice. The students were all success stories, and happy they had made that decision themselves.

I learned that many of the foreign medical schools' classes for the fall were already filled. However, there was a medical school in Guadalajara, Mexico, that admitted students in the fall and the spring, so I could finish up my fall classes at the UM-College Park, move to Mexico in the spring, and start medical school there in the fall—assuming they would admit me.

I also heard that a friend of mine, Bob, was at medical school down at the Universidad Autónoma de Guadalajara (the Independent University of Guadalajara), which was a private school. I didn't know his number but called 411 and learned there was someone with his last name listed in Timonium, Maryland. I gave it a try and his mother answered the phone. She said I'd called the right house, and she was sure Bob would love to see me. In fact, he was home for the Christmas holidays. Would I like to come down and say hello?

I didn't tell her I hadn't seen Bob for two years and didn't know him all that well, and simply wrote down the address, hopped in my car, and showed up just as Bob and his family were finishing dinner at their dining room table. It was a little awkward barging in like that, but his mother was so sweet—and she apologized to Bob for not telling him about her invitation to me—that any tension quickly melted away.

"So what's it like?" I said as we each kicked back with a bottle of beer in his living room.

"What are your grades and MCAT scores?" he asked.

I filled him in.

He casually took a sip. "Yeah, you'll get in. No problem. You fly down in April—I'll research the dates and mail them to you—and do an interview. I'm sure they'll accept you on the spot. And you can get scholarships and loans. Classes start in the fall, so you can stay in Guadalajara for three months to take an intensive Spanish class for American students. And bring some fun money. It's really hopping down there, especially in summer with all the tourists," he explained.

"Thanks. That's incredible," I said, thrilled that my chutzpah had paid off. I'd had no idea he would be so helpful.

"Guadalajara is quite an experience," he said. "It's like the wild, wild west down there."

"Really? What does that mean?"

"Well, there's not much law enforcement, for example, but you'll see. You should come on down and you can see yourself. It's a fun place and a good school."

Yes, I had found my alternate route.

Chapter Nine

Rocky Mountain High

fter I left Bob's house, I started putting my plan into action. I didn't have to leave for Mexico until April 15, so I had the winter ahead of me. I could have taken some classes, or gotten a jump on learning Spanish, but neither was necessary. I had two dreams—to become a doctor and a ski bum. Did they have to be mutually exclusive? I was on my way to making the first one come true. Maybe this hole in my schedule should be filled by an interlude where I would do nothing but ski.

It was the mid-seventies and one of the coolest places to be if you were in your twenties was Boulder, Colorado, and the surrounding areas. Boulder was the setting of the hit TV sitcom *Mork and Mindy*, featuring Robin Williams. Steamboat Springs, a nearby town that was originally built around ranches but became a ski resort and tourist town, was booming as well. I phoned my brother, who had graduated from college and moved to Steamboat Springs. He had flown there himself after receiving his instructor pilot's license—he'd gotten the flying bug from my dad. Rusty was living in Steamboat with friends and told me there was a housing shortage because of the boom in tourism, so if you had a place to stay, you could easily get a job—and spend your free time skiing. Why didn't I come out and join him?

I could just imagine hopping off a ski lift chair at the top of one of the hills and taking the black diamond course to the bottom only to repeat it over and over again. I was in. Well, I had to clear it with my parents. They supported me, which I really appreciated.

Bill, one of my roommates from Washington and Lee, had taken a year off before starting his MBA program at the University of Rochester, so I called him up and asked him if he would be interested in spending the winter months in Steamboat Springs after the first of the year. He was all for it, so in a few days, he drove his Subaru station wagon, which we called the Bu, down to Hampstead, Maryland, to pick me up and we headed west.

When we got to Steamboat Springs, we found jobs at a condominium maintenance company called Storm Meadows. They managed 235 condos and 13 townhouses right on the slopes. You could actually walk outside of your condo, put on your skis, and walk over to the ski lift.

Bill and I were hired as wood handlers: Our job was to deliver firewood from a big pile to the condo balconies so people could enjoy roaring fires in their fireplaces. We could have chosen to be housemen, who cleaned up the common areas between the condos, but since that was a more public job, they had a rule that you couldn't have a beard. It was cold and beards were in style, so we went for the wood handler jobs instead. Besides, I knew once I got to Mexico I would have to shave and cut my hair as those were the rules in medical school. Long hair and beards on men were still very "out there" as far as the older generation was concerned. They could put up with our bell-bottom blue jeans, which we paired with clingy men's shirts, but the hairy look was a little too much, I guess.

Quickly, I realized that wood handling tied me up during the day and I really wanted to ski, so after a week, I sacrificed my beard to be a houseman. Now, I was working 7:00 to 9:00 a.m. and 3:00 p.m. to

7:00 p.m. six days a week. Those were great hours for somebody who was there to ski.

Bill and I stayed with Rusty and his friends for a night or two and then learned that Steamboat Springs College had extra dorm rooms they rented out to Storm Meadows employees for $80 a month, which was a fantastic bargain from our perspective. Because it was just a dorm room, we only had access to a hotplate and toaster—no refrigerator and no microwave, as those had not yet become common. Cooking meals would turn out to be problematic. The restaurants on Main Street catered to wealthy tourists, and the sandwiches on hearty bread and loaded up with alfalfa sprouts were very tasty but too expensive as far as I was concerned. Bill and I made a lot of powdered soup mixed with boiling water in a mug. We also found some backstreet burger joints on side streets that were affordable.

Recreational drug use was more common than ever, especially in a town like Steamboat Springs. Pot was readily available, and I decided to indulge in it as much as I could because I wouldn't be able to enjoy it once I got to Mexico. I had seen the movie *Midnight Express,* based on a true story of an American guy who made the mistake of trying to smuggle some hashish out of Turkey for recreational use back home. He was caught and ended up in a nightmare prison scenario far from the reach of the U.S. government. With that horrifying possibility in my head, I wasn't going to touch any drug but alcohol once I got to Mexico.

Cocaine seemed to be in fashion, but it was way out of my price range. I only used it a few times—when someone else paid for it. I was up for some drug adventures, though, so I said yes to some mescaline-laced chocolate one day, which was a fun high but definitely not something I wanted to do when socializing because you go into your own world— more so than with marijuana.

As always, I was reliable when it came to my obligations, so I took it seriously when I was promoted to supervisor of the housemen after a couple of weeks. Bill had been promoted as well—to a position in the office—because like me, he was a college grad. Just about all the fellows who worked there were "taking a year off from college," and everyone was pretty sure they weren't going to find themselves back on campus when they could hang out at a ski resort indefinitely, doing easy jobs and skiing every day. The half dozen housemen quickly revolted against me because I told them that they couldn't hide among the towels and sheets in the linen closets in the condo buildings and sleep or read paperback novels. They pointed out that I'd sneaked off to do the same thing when I was a houseman, and I said, "Yeah, but I didn't do it until the work was done." They grumbled and glared at me until the day came when I used my passkey to get into an empty condo where the maintenance man had reported there was a batch of pot brownies that had been left behind in the refrigerator. I took custody of them and doled them out among the other fellows. Their opinions of me changed after that.

Drugs were so acceptable there that one morning at the end of February, when I took a gondola ride to the top of one of the ski hills, the fellow sitting next to me lit up a joint and offered it to me. It was about 9:00 a.m. Maybe this was his version of coffee? I said, "No thanks." It was a little early in the day to get high, I thought.

I hopped off the gondola at the top of the mountain and headed over to a ski run called White Out, a short expert run at the top, and began making my way down. As I got close to the bottom, I noticed some people at the bottom standing there watching us skiers. They seemed to be cheering me on and I decided to show off a bit as I went over the bumps—the local term for moguls. I was getting lots of air each time and then suddenly, I lost my balance, fell backward, and caught my skis. The ski boots I was wearing went higher up the calf than modern ones do, so when the boot slipped beneath me as I fell backward, I felt a sharp pain— and knew instantly that I had broken something.

On my first run of the day!

I put my skis in the snow, forming a cross, to signal the ski patrol, and waited there in the snow until they came a few minutes later. When I told them what happened, they said, "Yes, it sounds like you've injured something, but we're really busy. You're not far from the bottom. Usually, the White Out skiers can make it down on their own if they get injured…" I got the hint. They thought I ought to suck it up like everyone else did. I didn't say, "Listen, I'm pretty sure I broke something." Instead, I said dully,

"Yeah, sure, no problem." I managed to get up with their help and tried to salvage my pride as I snowplowed down to the bottom, wincing with pain the whole way.

I immediately went to ski patrol building, where they examined me and determined I had better take their makeshift ambulance to the nearest emergency room. At the hospital, they gave me an X-ray and told me I might have a broken bone, but they wanted to call in an orthopedic surgeon to examine me. When he showed up, he looked at the X-ray and measured the distance from the outside of my ankle bone up to the point where it looked like it was a fracture line. He walked over to me, put his finger on the outside of my ankle, and pressed in on my thigh at the point where the fracture line appeared to be. "Ouch!" I yelped.

"It's broken," he pronounced.

Ugh! Maybe I should've taken the joint! I knew if I'd been high, I would have been more mellow and less anxious—less tempted to try to impress strangers with my skiing.

"Are you going to want to ski anymore this season?" he asked.

"Yeah, absolutely. That's why I came out here."

"Well, I won't put a cast on you, but you have to be careful so that you don't snap the bone. It's just a fracture line in the fibula."

I knew that a fibula isn't a weight-bearing bone, so as long as I didn't do something dumb like stand on tiptoe, I'd be fine with just an Ace bandage, which was the only other option. "Okay," I said. So much for my stint as a ski bum!

I still had several weeks to go before I would leave for Mexico, so I started working more and saving money. That night, I took some Percocets that I'd been prescribed in the ER and went out dancing at a disco, although I couldn't get around the dance floor very well. I kept my left leg straight as I rotated my right leg and tipped my right hand to drink beer. I liked the buzz the combination of beer and Percocets gave me. I also noticed that the beer didn't make me tired—maybe the painkillers counteracted the side effect of the alcohol? And I felt fine the next day—well, except for the throbbing pain in my leg, but I had more Percocets for that.

I got bored pretty quickly, and boredom seemed like a good excuse for me to become a party animal every night. Drink, pop Percocets, party all night—that was my pattern for the next five weeks.

I planned a cross-country ski trip with my friends and brother because I figured I could handle that gentler form of skiing. The morning we were supposed to leave, a friend handed me a package of freeze-dried psilocybin—hallucinogenic mushrooms—and said, "Chew on these! They're supposed to be great." He was not referring to the taste. In fact, they tasted like dried grass mixed with cow manure. They probably were mixed with cow manure. But I was up for an adventure, so I grimaced, chewed, swallowed, and waited to see what kind of high I would experience.

Rusty picked us up as planned, and we started driving around looking for the hot springs for which Steamboat Springs was named—apparently, the early European explorers heard the hissing of the hot steam and thought it was the sound of nearby steamboats. Rusty made a wrong turn and ended up on a road where there was an open pasture on the hillside, where a couple dozen or so elks were standing in the field. Normally, I would be excited by the site of so many majestic wild animals, but something was off. They seemed to be mannequins, or frozen, or maybe sculptures. And they were staring at us! Every one of them! I was mesmerized. And then I realized the effect of the "magic mushrooms" had kicked in.

We soon found the trailhead for the hot springs and got out and put on our cross-country boots and skis. We trekked back on our cross-country skis across frozen Steamboat Lake, and then skied our way into a wooded area and started down a switchback. At last, we found a spot where you could see the steam coming up off rocks where hot watered trickled off of them into pools of water that ran into other pools. Hsssssss. There were at least fifty people in groups of three, four, or more sitting in the water, filling every pool. And everyone was naked.

We headed down to the waterside, sampled the wine and cheese someone laid out, and stood there fully clothed until someone pointed out a couple of pretty girls our age coming down the mountain. That was our signal. Lucky for us, one of the pools had just emptied so we peeled off our clothes and jumped into the water naked, hoping that the girls would make their way toward us. Sure enough, the girls came down to the pools. As they chatted away, they took off their skis, boots, down vests, jeans, sweaters and socks—oh, this was getting better and better—their bras, and finally, their panties. Then, they began to walk toward us. I swallowed hard as they lowered themselves into the pool with us as if they did this every day. High as I was, I managed to act as if this were the most natural experience in the world. Oh, I was cool.

It was fun, and weird, and after those girls left, I got, well, water logged, so I stepped out of the water and got dressed again. Then I noticed my boss, Randy, from Storm Meadows was there with his wife. They were naked. Randy's wife saw me, waved, and started walking toward us.

"Anyone up for some pecan pie? I just baked it," she said. "I can go get it from the car!"

I love pecan pie to this day…

Finally, my leg healed enough so that I could ski in early April. Steamboat Springs had just been dumped with 12 inches of champagne powder so dry and soft you can sweep it up in your hand, blow on it, and watch the champagne-like spritz you create. I was able to put my boots on and take a run down the powder-covered mountain. After two more runs, my leg hurt very badly, so I had to stop. That ended up being the last skiing in Steamboat for me. It was absolutely the best day I had of skiing that winter. I had finally met my goal and mastered powder skiing. That was something I never could have done out on the east coast where the snow is generally more wet and dense and quickly turns to what the locals call "hard-packed powder"—known in Colorado as "ice." I love the east coast, but there is no comparison to skiing in Colorado.

The next day, I packed up my stuff and waved good-bye to my friend Bill, who took me to the airport. I remember the plane accelerating down the runway and me looking out the window at the mountains as we flew south. I thought, *Well, I'm headed to Mexico. My life as I know it is over.*

Chapter Ten   Guadalajara

P arty time was over. I needed to buckle down and get into the study mode again.

I had tried to call Bob to let him know when my flight was, as he had offered to meet my plane, but his landline wasn't working. Phone service in Mexico in those days was somewhat spotty. I decided to take a risk and send him a telegram, and then get on the flight and cross my fingers.

I brought with me enough money from my parents to pay for my living expenses until the fall and for the tuition for the intensive Spanish course. They also gave me enough money for a down payment toward medical school tuition. The chicken raising business had worked out very well for dad, and I was very grateful to them. I was also grateful to Bob, who had told me everything I needed to know to get myself into the medical school.

After I landed and walked off the plane, I immediately spotted him, which made me relax a bit. In fact, I broke into a big smile as I saw him, because I certainly couldn't have missed him in the crowd. At six feet tall, he would have stood out even if he wasn't wearing aviator glasses and a tan cowboy hat. We said hello and I stepped back to see he was wearing an ordinary white shirt, khaki pants, and some very high-end cowboy boots that I had to comment on. "Handmade leather," he bragged. "The exchange rate is twenty-five pesos to a dollar. Couldn't pass these up."

It occurred to me that my money would stretch a long way in Mexico. Even so, I wasn't going to go shopping, but I was planning to have some fun—work hard, play hard was working for me. Bob and I grabbed my luggage, threw it in his Volkswagen station wagon, and headed out.

We drove around the Periférico, which is the highway that surrounds Guadalajara, and then Bob made a left turn from the far right, crossing in front of six lanes of oncoming traffic. Noticing that I had just tensed up at his crazy maneuver, he said, "Ah, don't worry about it. It's just how they drive down here. Everyone does it."

I asked if this was what he meant when he'd said it was "the wild west" in Guadalajara, and he explained, "The cops here are busy. They don't have time for the small stuff. If you're loud, rowdy, breaking a few things here and there—they don't care. We're *gueros*—rich, white American guys—they don't pay us much mind."

Bob turned out to be a great host. He put me up in his apartment, which was in a nice part of Guadalajara called Chapalita where many retirees lived because the prices were incredibly cheap and the weather was beautiful year 'round.

The very next day, he drove me to my interview and as expected, I was accepted on the spot. I walked over to another office on campus to enroll in the three-month intensive Spanish course that would meet five times a week for six hours a day. The class didn't start though for two weeks, so I had some free time to kill.

Back at Bob's, I met a few of his friends, and they told me that the coming weekend was going to be the start of spring break for the med school students. Bob said his plan was to join his friend Ed in driving to California in Ed's Fiat Spider. Here I was in Mexico, knowing only the

Spanish I had taken for three years in high school, and Bob said, "Why don't you take my car and use my apartment while I'm gone for the week?"

I was stunned at my good fortune. I had made a commitment that I was going to experience Mexico rather than study every waking moment, so of course I said, "Thanks!" and took his set of keys. But the next day after Bob left, I sat on one of his beat-up chairs that was coved by a thick, cheap, cotton Mexican blanket and wondered what I was going to do all week, with little skill at speaking Spanish, no one to navigate for me, and lots of money in my pocket.

Bob's landline was working again, so I called up his friend Rocco, who was from Pittsburgh, who had told me that he was going to stay in town and that his sister Olivia would be visiting. He said that he and some friends were going to a disco called The Blackout that night and I was welcome to join them. I told him I remembered seeing it when Bob drove me past the university, and I'd meet them in a few hours.

I hung up, took out a bottle of wine from Bob's wine rack, opened it, and settled down with a glass of merlot and a Spanish dictionary to look up some phrases that I felt could come in handy: "¿Quieres bailar?" which means, "Do you want to dance?" "¿Quieres algo de tomar?" which is, "Do you want something to drink?" "Lo siento," because I was sure I was going to embarrass myself and have to say, "I'm sorry." (Which is what "Lo siento" means.)

I didn't really have any experience speaking Spanish, much less to native speakers, and it had been six years since I'd taken third year Spanish, but I felt prepared. Off I went to Blackout.

I had plenty of pesos, but Rocco and his pretty brunette sister Olivia and I were getting our drinks paid for by a Mexican millionaire named Rafael Rodriguez, who was trying to impress Olivia by throwing money around. While he worked on getting her to be more than just cordial to him, I started asking girls to dance with me on the elevated part of the stage floor. I had no problem finding girls who would get up on the dance floor with me. A few hours later, I was quite happily intoxicated when I stepped off of the dance floor right on one of the small tables next to it. I lost my balance, the table tipped, and I came down with a crash. "Lo siento," I said to the people around me. Yep, that was a good phrase to have memorized.

This was a wonderful introduction to Mexico for me. Day two, I took a twenty-minute flight to Puerto Vallarta with Rocco, Olivia, and their new friend, the macho Rafael, to join Rafael's wealthy family who was vacationing at the famous tropical paradise and fishing village on Mexico's west coast. We took a cab to the Camino Real and I discovered that Rafael had a room for Olivia and him and a room for Rocco and me. Apparently, she was okay with that. We met Rafael later that afternoon and he had rented a six-seat boat that was like a taxi to take us out to a little island for lunch at a restaurant on the water. As I sat back watching the sun dance on the water, feeling the balmy breeze while I drank a cold Corona under the palapa, or thatch-covered shelter, on the beach, I thought, *I can't believe I'm here!* I hadn't really thought about how much fun Mexico would be. When I left Steamboat Springs, it felt as if my life as I knew it was over, but this new chapter was looking good.

The waiters brought out red snapper—huachinango—which Rafael had ordered for the table. When I looked at it, I saw they had simply jabbed a stick into its mouth, cut its back along its spine, gutted it, and grilled it on the skewer over an open charcoal fire. I thought, *Now, I can't be rude and not eat this, but I really have absolutely no interest in eating fish, much less when it's staring at me with lifeless eyes.* I made myself try it anyway. It tasted fantastic. Now, I actually prefer fish over any other type of meat. That memorable meal totally flipped my opinion about eating fish.

That night, Rafael took us to Carlos O'Brien's restaurant, which is very well known in Puerto Vallarta, and we had another magnificent meal. Rafael seemed to know everyone and the place was packed because it was a holiday in Mexico. And after that, we were off to a popular disco called the City Dump, which was celebrating their seventh anniversary as a nightclub with a big, open party. But that wasn't enough. We bar hopped over to the City Dump where Rafael was easily able to get us past the gold cord that separated the VIPs from the crowds of people who wanted to get in but didn't know anyone important enough to help them jump the line.

At the City Dump, I met a girl named Lupita. I thought her name was both beautiful and exotic, but later learned that just about every girl was named Lupita, short for Guadalupe, the patron saint of Mexico—just like almost every guy was named Jesus. Lupita would become my girlfriend for a few months.

I started the intensive Spanish program and began to travel by three buses to meet Lupita on the other side of Guadalajara whenever I could. It didn't bother me that I had no car. I was totally open to the experience, and there were plenty of buses running all the time because many people in Mexico couldn't afford cars. Guadalajara had a population of several million. In fact, it was one of the biggest cities in Mexico, second only to Mexico City. I peered at the posted maps, hopped on the bus, grabbed the overhead railing if I didn't have a seat, or even fell asleep as I bumped up against the passengers sitting next to me. Occasionally, people would bring their chickens and produce onto the bus, which didn't bother me. I was used to poultry squawking and flapping. Besides, I wouldn't be in Mexico if it weren't for our family's chickens back home.

Meanwhile, I developed a taste for the local food, which was quite different from Tex-Mex food, except for the jalapeños. And I learned about the custom of American students renting an apartment, buying the furniture, and selling it to another American student who came to rent the apartment when the school year ended. I discovered a very nice penthouse apartment on the third floor of a building and knew it would be perfect for me. It had two bedrooms and sliding glass doors that opened on to a wraparound patio that overlooked the city of Guadalajara. There were no screens though, so the student who had rented the place before me had rigged a mosquito net over the bed. I soon discovered that if I kept a fan blowing over me all night, it would keep the mosquitoes from landing on me, so I was able to yank down the ugly rigging and wake up free of bug bites. That didn't solve the cockroach problem, though. One night, I woke up when I felt a big one crawling across my face.

I was starting to meet other medical students thanks to the Spanish class, and socializing with Bob a lot. Another fellow had picked up a cute little Cocker Spaniel named Pecos that I would bend down to pet whenever I saw him in the courtyard. Pecos was still a puppy, so he would gnaw on my hand, but I didn't mind and neither did any of Bob's other friends—that is, until I went to Bob's one day and discovered that Pecos had been put down because he developed rabies.

"You're kidding me, right?" I said.

"Sorry, 'fraid not," said Bob.

No one survives rabies, so if you've been exposed, you have to get a series of fourteen shots of anti-rabies vaccine. They give you the shots in your belly, and they're incredibly painful and leave big red welts. All the other fellows who needed the treatment were the wealthy sons of doctors, so they simply had their fathers ship them boxes of the vaccine from back home, which they could inject themselves. This was a purer form of the vaccine than was available in the local clinics, which provided free healthcare to Mexicans and hapless Americans like me. Lupita and I went into one and I watched as a nurse injected one child with something, wiped the hypodermic needle off on a cloth, use it to inject the next child, and so on. Although I couldn't afford to have high quality rabies vaccine shipped down to me from America, I had the money for some clean, disposable needles—so Lupita and I provided them each time we went in for our shots. Fortunately, the AIDS epidemic was long into the future, so those kids probably didn't get ill, even with the unsanitary condition of the needles used on them.

Before classes began in the fall, I found a roommate to take the second bedroom. Jimmy was a very bright fellow from New Jersey who had graduated from high school at fifteen and from college when he was eighteen. His parents were both physicians, which I would soon find was common among the medical students. Jimmy told me that he had planned to be a workaholic like his Irish-immigrant father until Jimmy turned eighteen and his dad, who was only thirty-eight, had a heart attack that almost killed him. Sobered by his father nearly dying, Jimmy decided to slow down. He started thinking about his life and realized that despite his success as a professional martial arts competitor and boxer, he wanted to become a doctor. He had gone back to graduate school and then come to

Guadalajara. I was glad to find someone who was very serious about school but a lot of fun, too.

School started and for the first two weeks, I tried to figure out how I was going to study. Despite the three years of high school Spanish and the intensive three-month course, I was having trouble remembering vocabulary words. The Spanish textbooks had English versions I could study from, but that left the challenge of taking exams in Spanish. Finally, I realized that if I spent the day before a test translating all the English medical terms into Spanish and memorized them, I could do well on the Spanish-language exam the next day. This approach worked well enough to earn me As in all of my classes.

I continue with that impressive performance for the entire first year. With no sports to distract me like they had when I was as an undergraduate, or when I was doing non-degree graduate work and hanging out in the bars watching sports, I found it easier to focus on my studies.

My mind was really clear. The time I'd spent skiing made me realize that although I loved the pure joy of skiing, I needed some purpose to my life. Skiing was a nice lark, but I wanted to be of service to other people. I was on my way to meeting that goal.

Many of my fellow students wanted to become doctors because that's what their physician parents expected of them. They didn't share my passion for becoming a healer. Because they weren't totally committed to the path that had been carved out for them by their parents', they didn't earn the grades or test scores to get into American medical school. Many were embarrassed and hoped to win their parents' approval by doing well in Guadalajara. They seemed to walk around with clouds of failure of over their heads and were a pretty unhappy group. My perspective and motivation were completely different. I was glad to have Jimmy and Bob as friends, because they understood me and why I was serious about doing well.

One of these students carrying the weight of her parents' expectations was a Jewish girl from Long Island—Sarah, who had a boyfriend back in the United States. I had a girlfriend back home named Lynn, and I had dated Lupita for a while but that relationship wasn't very serious, and it was winding down. Sarah wasn't looking to get involved and neither was I. We spent a lot of time with each other studying and talking about our lives. I was attracted to her, but saw her as a friend for now. I felt a little guilty about cheating on Lynn with Lupita, but Lynn was caught up in the social scene at college, and we hadn't made any promises to each other. For all I knew, she wasn't faithful to me either. It was a transitional time in both our lives, and I was young, so I didn't know how to clarify the situation without a lot of tears and drama on her part. I didn't want to hurt Lynn's feelings. Sarah might become a girlfriend or might not—and I figured I could officially break it off with Lynn back home when and if that happened. In retrospect, I probably should have been clear with every one of my girlfriends, but it didn't seem all that important at the time. Keeping everyone happy was the priority, and that meant keeping silent about what was really going on with me and other girls.

I'm glad Sarah and I were just friends at first. She had a big influence on me. Having a female friend I could talk to at length about serious matters helped reinforce my commitment to focus on studying and kept me away from chasing girls like Lupita who just wanted to hang out in clubs and have fun. Later, Sarah and I would become lovers—and by that time, Lynn and I had drifted apart and there was no need for an emotional phone call breaking it off officially.

I was into the momentum of school again, studying hard, but when the weekend came, it was time to play hard. And Guadalajara was a fantastic place to do that.

Chapter Eleven

Cars and Craziness

B efore I returned to Guadalajara for the second year of medical school, my parents, who were upgrading to a new car, decided to give me their 1975 grey Caprice station wagon. I loved that car. You could lower the window in the back with the push of a button, and there were seats in the back where you could look backwards. You could fit nine or ten people in that boat of a vehicle. Even so, most of the time when I went out with my pals, we ended up in my friend Ed's huge blue Chrysler—the one he and Bob had taken to California the year before. The late seventies' cars were gas guzzlers, but gas was still pretty cheap back then in both the U.S. and Mexico—even though we groused about the prices that had risen close to a dollar a gallon.

Like me, Ed took studying seriously. He was a bit rough around the edges, from a working class home in West Hartford, Connecticut, and he cussed a lot, but that didn't bother a hayseed like me. Along with our friend Bob, who was even crazier than we were when it came to late night partying, and Pat, a good looking, athletic, Italian guy who was a magnet for the Mexican ladies, we would make our way after hours to Zona Roja, the red-light district that was filled with bars, clubs for drinking and dancing, and even brothels. Zona Roja stayed open until 3:00 a.m., so we would carry on our carousing for a few more hours before heading back to our apartments to sleep it off.

Zona Roja was well guarded by men in military uniforms who would search you for firearms before you paid your admission to enter a discotheque. The clubs weren't officially brothels, and at first, we thought they were all just bars. But we soon learned that many of the pretty girls who showed interest in us were only checking us out as potential customers. They brought men upstairs after cutting a business deal. I had some awkward endings to conversations before I figured out that I was less charming and attractive than I liked to think I was, and that many of the ladies expressing an interest in me were actually only interested in the pesos in my wallet.

One particular night, we had met as usual at someone's apartment and begun drinking and swapping stories. Pat, Ed, Bob, and I were up for an adventure so we headed out to the bars.

Around 3:00 a.m., we decided we had better head back home from Zona Roja. We piled into Ed's big blue Chrysler: Bob rode shotgun and I got into the back with Pat. We had been drinking for hours but were reasonably sober, or so we believed. Your judgment slips away after about the third cerveza (beer—that was another Spanish term that came in handy for me).

There were a lot of stop signs and intersections at the end of Zona Roja, where we turned to go back toward the university. At this time of night, when the roads were pretty deserted, people would slow down at intersections and then just head on through without stopping at stop signs. They treated them more as suggestions than warnings because there were few police to enforce the traffic laws. Ed approached each intersection with a certain amount of caution. He certainly didn't want to get into an accident in Guadalajara. For one thing, only about ten percent of people carried auto insurance, so if he banged up the Chrysler, he would have to pay for it. Plus, when the police came upon a car accident, their usual response was to arrest the drivers, put them in jail, and then sort out who was responsible for the damages and expenses later on when they had time to worry about the details. The American students figured out that it was very important to carry insurance because if they got into an accident and were found to be culpable, they would get stuck in jail until they could come up with the money to pay for the damages. That meant sitting behind bars until the driver got estimates and all the paperwork went through, and believe me, you did *not* want to get stuck in a Mexican jail for days, much less weeks. Given that most Mexicans didn't have insurance, money, or the patience to sort out matters after an accident, most of them would drive away as quickly as possible after a collision.

Bob had more or less drifted off to sleep. Ed was cussing right and left, angry that some girl at the disco had rejected him after he'd spent a lot of money on her. Soon, he was not even slowing down when he came up on a stop sign at 40 miles an hour in what was a 25-mile-per-hour zone.

Suddenly, I saw a flash of a vehicle out of the corner of my right eye as it entered the intersection in front of us. I heard the crunch of metal and flew forward, my violent motion stopped by the back of the front seat. I was bruised, as was everyone else, but fortunately, no one went through the windshield or out the door despite the fact that we weren't seat-belted in (airbags were very rare back then). The Chrysler may have guzzled a lot of gasoline, but it was built like a tank when it came to layers of metal between us and other cars.

I looked out the front window and saw a Volkswagen Beetle with a mangled door. We were on the left side of the road, the hood of our car was buckled, and I could hear the pssssshhhh of escaping steam.

For a moment, all of us were silent, taking in what had just happened. Bob was awake now, that's for sure. Then, Pat said, "Gee, Ed. What do you do in a situation like this in Mexico?"

Ed turned his head to glare at him from the front seat and said, "Just shut up. Just shut the fuck up and watch." He threw the car into reverse to separate us from the car we had just driven up onto the curb, turned the wheel sharply, and hit the gas to propel the Chrysler forward. I could see the driver in the other car get out—fortunately, he looked unharmed. The sound of his voice shouting, "Cabrones! Cabrones!"—Bastards!—began to fade as we sped forward down the road.

The Chrysler's headlights were pointing straight down at the road, so we couldn't see much ahead of us. Steam was rolling out of the damaged radiator and I wondered if the engine would overheat before we got back to our side of town. When we reached the top of the hill near Ed's place, the engine stalled. Pat, Bob, and I got out to push as Ed steered it to the front of his house.

The next morning, we reported a hit and run. Everyone was okay, except for a bump on Bob's head when he hit the windshield on the original impact. Lucky for him, he had a hard head.

And lucky for me, I still had that Caprice station wagon from my parents. So while Ed's car was out of commission, we had wheels to take to Zona Rosa again.

Another night, we were driving to the famous red-light district when we came to an intersection. I pulled up behind a big blue station wagon with California plates that had zoomed past me and quickly cut in front of me. Although it was dark, I could see that the back window was rolled down and at least half a dozen Mexican guys with long black hair were hanging out the back of the car as well as out of the sides.

The driver got out, came up to the window, and angrily started banging on it. I looked over at my friend and roommate Jimmy and said, "What's his problem?"

Jimmy said, "I don't know. Maybe you cut him off or something?" We were puzzled, but I was in no mood to roll down my window and let this furious guy take a swing at me through an open window. I stayed in place and the light turned green.

I said to Jimmy, "Well, I'm just going to go around him." I pulled to the left and kind of bumped the guy who was standing there at my window. Then, I drove around his car and kept going down the road.

The next thing I knew, the blue station wagon full of men was pulling up next to us on our left. I could see the driver was angrier than he was before. He was shaking his fist at us and swearing loudly in Spanish. I realized I was in a road race with him on El Calle, which has six lanes of traffic—three in each direction. The guy bumped his car against mine, and I held on to the wheel to keep from going off the road on the right. I drove faster and he fell behind.

I definitely felt intimidated. When we came up toward the next intersection, he was able to pull up in front of me, which blocked my ability to drive forward. I had cars behind me so I couldn't back up to escape, and I couldn't turn right without going over the sidewalk because I was in the far right lane.

The driver jumped out again, and was banging even harder on my window than he had the first time. I said to Jimmy, "We're going to have to get out and fight. Let's get out your side."

Jimmy started to get out of the car and the driver ran around the other side to confront him. As he did, Jimmy threw a bottle of Bohemian beer at the fellow's forehead. It bounced off, and Jimmy grabbed the fellow's hair and ran him into the stone wall on the opposite side of the sidewalk. Rule number one: Don't piss off an inebriated guy who used to be a professional boxer and karate fighter.

As I got out, a second fellow came flying over the hood of the car. Remembering what Jimmy had taught me about boxing—"just in case you ever need it"—I got into a fistfight with him. Then, a third guy came out of the car toward us with a screwdriver in his hand. He tried to stab Jimmy, but Jimmy blocked him with a karate move and threw the fellow away from him. Then, Jimmy jumped in the car, which was still running, and scooted over to the driver's seat.

Traffic had cleared out now. He yelled, "Get in!" I jumped back into the car and tried to dodge as one of the guys punched at me through the door as I was closing it, cutting my eye. He backed up and the guy with the screwdriver jumped on the hood of the car. He started beating on it and cracked the windshield. Jimmy threw the Caprice into reverse and hit the gas. The force threw the guy off the hood of the car. He jumped up and ran into his car, Jimmy started to pull up on the fellow's left side to pass him, and the guy put his car in reverse and rammed the front of our car, bending our right front fender as we started driving away.

Jimmy didn't stop. The other car continued to ram the side of my car and dented the front door, back door, and rear fenders on my car's right hand side. The driver of the other car never got up to chase us, so we zoomed off.

Jimmy drove us back to my apartment as fast as he could. We parked the car so it looked like a hit and run, and that's how we reported it. It meant parking on the wrong side of the street so we could claim someone hit the car's right side, but the police didn't question it. That's just the way these things were handled in Guadalajara.

Chapter Twelve   # The Bubble

I t was spring break, and my friend Bob and his girlfriend Barb spontaneously decided to take a trip from Guadalajara to Las Hadas in Manzanillo. Las Hadas is a high-end resort best known as the place where they filmed the famous scene in the movie *10* where Dudley Moore, who is lusting after the bikini-wearing Bo Derek, throws towels on the scorching beach sand as he walks. I was looking forward to the sun and sand and had some money to burn thanks to the allowance my father was giving me and to my own frugality. Bob had inherited money from his grandmother, and we figured that between us and his girlfriend, we could split the costs of staying there for the week: just $200. We packed a cooler with a fifth of vodka and some tomato juice, hot sauce, and Worcestershire sauce for Bloody Marys among the ice cubes.

The three of us drove in Bob's car for four hours before we arrived in Manzanillo and checked in. We were driven by golf cart from the parking lot to our two-bedroom villa, with a terrace that looked out at the villas, restaurants, and pools that dotted the hillside at the edge of the cliffs. The resort was filled with many Americans and Canadians sipping cool drinks with umbrellas and spears of olives.

That first night, we had a late dinner at a resort restaurant and enjoyed the view from the terrace. At one point, I asked the waiter, "¿Dónde está el baño?" which is, "Where is the bathroom?" He pointed me in the general direction of the bathroom at the back of the tiny nightclub I would walk through. Inebriated as I was, I felt certain I was able to walk as if completely sober. By this time, I had a lot of practice faking sobriety. My focus was on my feet and looking nonchalant so no one would guess at my true condition. I passed the grand piano on my right hand side, and barely noticed the lady with the long, blonde, curly locks who was sitting at the keyboard playing quietly for the few couples as they sat and talked softly. I returned along the same route, finished dinner with Bob and his girlfriend, and went to bed.

The next morning, I went to a buffet breakfast featuring a big, beautiful display of fresh fruits, pastries, and breads. I really was quite hung-over and hoped a little hydration from juice and water would help as I waited for Bob and Barb to join me. The waiter poured hot coffee into my cup and said, "So were you at the bar last night?"

"Yeah," I said. "For a minute."

"Did you see her?"

I squinted up at his face, which was bright with excitement. He was a Mexican fellow, around my age. "Stevie Nicks! Fleetwood Mac rented a private village with their own pool up on the side of the hill. They just completed a new album, and Stevie was in the lounge playing piano last night. Do you know Fleetwood Mac and Stevie Nicks?"

My heart sank. "Yeah, sure. She's great. They're great. Must have missed them."

"Too bad. What an opportunity, right?" He smiled and I nodded while inwardly kicking myself. I absolutely loved Stevie Nicks, the lead singer of the band. She was my dream date—the celebrity I would most like to hang out with. In my fantasy, I would be her down-to-earth boyfriend that she confided in and spent long nights with under the stars. And now it turns out I'd walked right by her thanks to my tunnel vision and my need not to trip over myself in my drunkenness. Damn!

After our weekend, I went back to class and by the end of that first year I was in a good place. I'd earned straight As, I was playing American football on the local team—it was a casual enough game that it took little time out of my schedule. I was boxing here and there, which was a fun little hobby.

And the drinking? Part of the addiction is the freedom and sense of euphoria that comes from being buzzed. It's a fleeting feeling, and I craved it. I needed to experience blissful nothingness, and the only way I knew how to do that was with alcohol—well, alcohol or sex. Sarah and I were having a lot of that until she told her parents about me. They flipped out because I wasn't Jewish, and she gave into the pressure to break up with me.

As for the alcohol, in retrospect, I got out of control on the weekends when I was partying, but it didn't feel that way to me. I told myself I was a long way from the unpredictable, over-the-top aggression I felt those few times in high school when I drank—and I told myself that even then, it was dark or hard liquor to blame. The explanation didn't make much sense if you looked at it closely, but I told myself it did. I could twist the details around to fashion a plausible excuse for why it was okay for me to drink as much as I did now. One of those excuses was that I was a good person. To me, good people didn't get drunk and do ugly things, or put their drinking and drugging ahead of other people's needs. I was a good person, not a sloppy drunk, or a self-centered drug addict manipulating his friends or stealing from other people. The stereotypes of drug and alcohol users I was familiar with reassured me that I wasn't in the same category as they were and never would be.

One day, when I was driving near one of the canals around Guadalajara, I saw a Mustang ahead of me in the opposite lane. On its roof were what looked like small jewelry display boxes. As the car turned right, moving away from me, I noticed out of the corner of my eye that some of the boxes flew off. I stopped as soon as I could, assessed the traffic, and hurried over to scoop them up. Peering around, I didn't see the Mustang. I carefully opened one of the boxes and saw what appeared to be a diamond necklace. What did I know, though? Maybe it was a cheap knockoff in a nice box. I opened the other boxes and found what looked like a pearl necklace and bracelet. Some of them had sparkly rings in them. I carried the boxes over to my car and put them on the passenger seat, made a U-turn, and then a right in the direction the Mustang had driven. Before I knew it, I saw it the Mustang ahead of me, parked. A Mexican woman with a worried expression was checking the road behind her.

Oh good, I thought. *Bet she'll be glad to see me!*

I stepped out of the car with a box in my hand and waved to get her attention. Her eyes grew wide and she hurried toward me, speaking Spanish quickly. I showed her the boxes in my passenger seat and opened the door. Her voice broke as she told me she had had just picked up her grandchild from daycare after stopping at a jewelry store. The jeweler had trusted her to take some of his inventory home to show her husband before she decided what to buy, and she'd placed the boxes on the roof of the car while settling the toddler into his seat. Then, she completely forgot about the boxes on her roof before driving away.

"It's all here," she said in Spanish. "This is $5,000 in jewelry! I can't believe you didn't just drive away like anyone else would. Here—" The tears began to roll down her cheeks as she reached for her wallet.

"No, no," I said. "It's no problem." She tried to insist that I take a handful of bills but it didn't feel right to me to take any money from her. She thanked me over and over again, and I felt great, knowing I had made her day and probably her year.

Being an addict doesn't suppress the goodness within you. It temporarily sequesters what you fear so you don't have to deal with it. It brings you into the moment artificially, as if ensconcing you safely in a bubble. And when you're in that bubble, you don't think about what you're doing and what the cost might be. You don't consider whether you're really okay to drive, or whether you might be hurting someone with one casual little lie after another. The uncomfortable truths are outside your bubble.

For me, there were several uncomfortable truths. I was sleeping with plenty of girls, and dodged their obvious attempts to get me to make a commitment to them or tell them if I was sleeping with anyone else. I had an addiction to emotional safety, to little white lies, and to playing it safe rather than doing what was hard emotionally. My bubble of reality floated gently above the ground, suspending my reality. From the inside, everything looked just fine.

I was starting to forget what it was like to be completely immersed in the moment, with senses fully awake, like I had experienced back on the farm when I was a kid. However, there was a day when I found myself playing softball in a field on a sunny and dusty mountain plateau in the desert near Guadalajara. We were all Japanese and American medical students, and since we didn't speak each others' languages, we communicated in Spanish. I remember sitting on the bench that served as the dugout, looking out at my fellow players, and thinking, *Wow, this will be a story I can share with my children and my grandchildren.*

Too often, though, I was lost in the haze of alcohol or drugs. One day, it was eating psilocybin mushrooms we'd plucked straight from cow patties and ingested without even rubbing the manure off of them—I guess the fact that I only got high, not sick, is a testament to my immune system. Another time it was margaritas at the beach. Ritalin was another drug I used in Mexico. Because it's so commonly prescribed for ADHD, it was becoming easily available, and many medical students used it to stay awake and focused while cramming for a test. Ritalin is a stimulant, and we crushed and snorted it. It had the nickname of "the poor man's cocaine." People liked it because it would keep you awake even when you were drinking. I can remember being so drunk that I just was ready to pass out, putting a straw under my nose with some Ritalin in a bowl that I had crushed, and snorting it. Then, almost as if somebody had blown a bugle, I woke up and thought, *Yeah! Let's keep going!*

I didn't use Ritalin to study. My study habits worked for me, so there was no need to alter them by altering my brain chemistry. But I did use Ritalin a few times to stay awake when I was drunk. I also tried a pharmaceutical amphetamine nicknamed black beauty, which combined amphetamine and dextroamphetamine and was used for weight loss. One of my friends from Tucson, Arizona, called them L.A. turnarounds because you could take a black beauty and put a case of beer in your car, drive to L.A., hang out a bit, and then turn around and drive home before the effects wore off. It was a 12-hour drive. Taking an L.A. turnaround early in the day would let me party all afternoon and into the night without disrupting my sleep or giving me a hangover the next day.

One Sunday morning in the springtime, I stopped by Bob's house to see what Bob and Ed were up to. They happened to be having strawberries and pancakes for breakfast, with champagne. At the end of the meal, we decided it was a good idea to smash our champagne glasses against the fireplace. And why not throw the plates as well? Okay, so there wasn't a fireplace, like there was in the movies when the hero gets mad and angrily pitches his empty glass into a roaring fire. We had to smash our dishes against a brick wall. It seemed hilarious at the time. In retrospect, it was a typical drunken behavior that reflected our sense of entitlement. Our attitude was hey, we worked hard, so we deserved to have some fun even if we were a little destructive. We could clean up the mess later.

As I recall, we left it for someone else to deal with.

Chapter Thirteen

Residency and a Serious Relationship

I spent three years enrolled in the medical school in Guadalajara, and by year three, I was logging a lot of time in the U.S. doing medical student rotations. All three years, I was keeping in contact with Dr. Willard Allen, the chairman of the Department of Admissions at the University of Maryland School of Medicine medical school, to get some guidance on how to ensure I would be admitted to their program. I knew that receiving a medical degree from the University of Maryland and an American medical school would give me more versatility when it came to a residency. Residents are matched up with hospitals based on the medical specialties they're most interested in, and at this point, I wanted to have several options to check out. The university I was at had too few specialty subjects, and I knew if I transferred, I would pretty much be guaranteed a surgical residency program in the United States. I wanted to become a surgeon anyway, but I thought it was important to keep an open mind, so I didn't want to close myself off to other possibilities.

After my first year of medical school in Mexico, Dr. Allen had recommended that I apply for transfer, which I did after taking part one of the medical boards and scoring well on them. Unfortunately, that year, there were no openings for transfer students. Still, I was determined to keep trying and keep my name in front of him. My second year, I again applied for transfer to the University of Maryland and that year they did accept six students in transfer, but I was informed by Dr. Allen I was the seventh person on that selection list. Ugh! I waited and waited, hoping someone would drop out and a position would open up, but I had no such luck. The third year, in the spring of 1982, I was doing clinical work in the United States in coordination with the medical school in Mexico when I again applied for transfer. I took a trip home and visited Dr. Allen in his office, where he looked me in the eye and said, "Steve, I have some good news and I have some bad news. The good news is I'm retiring and I'm looking forward to it. The bad news is for you. I'll be retiring before the admissions committee meets to consider the latest applications for transfer."

Yep, bad news was the way to describe it. Now what? I asked him who was going to be the new admissions chairman and he gave me her name. I decided I had better contact her and make an appointment so I could begin to build a relationship with her now that Dr. Allen was going to be out of the picture. I knew that if she met me face-to-face, I would stand out and that might give me an edge over other would-be transfer students. A resume and application is an inadequate snapshot of anyone, and I wanted her to actually experience how professional and committed I was.

I also decided it was time to contact Dr. Blanchard, an ear, nose and throat specialist that my mother had told me about. Years ago, my aunt had gone to him for her hearing issues and he had told her he was on the admissions committee. Fortunately, that little snippet of their conversation remained in her brain and she passed the information along to my mom who passed it along to me. I contacted Dr. Blanchard's office and made an appointment to introduce myself. He was a very kind older gentleman who didn't seem at all annoyed by my assertiveness in contacting him, but he was noncommittal, saying only, "I'll see what I can do." That was good enough for me. I intended to keep my name and face in front of him, too.

Then, before the week was over, I met with the chairman of the committee who gave me the same polite response.

About a week later, when I was enjoying a lacrosse game at Johns Hopkins University, I ran into Pat, an old friend from my Washington and Lee class. He was now playing professional basketball in Europe and was home in the U.S. for the summer. He asked what I was doing, so I told him about how I was studying medicine in Guadalajara but really wanted to transfer to the University of Maryland School of Medicine. "Oh, you should give my father a call. He's the Dean of the School of Medicine there! He likes Washington and Lee graduates." Now, what are the odds that I would run into someone who could connect me with yet another member of the University of Maryland School of Medicine who had the ability to influence the decision to accept my transfer? I believe my clear intention actually attracted that "coincidental" meeting with Pat. Very soon, I was sitting in Pat's father's office chatting. He, too, told me he would see would he could do for me.

I was optimistic, but I wanted to have a backup plan, too. I applied for a program at Maryland General Hospital in Baltimore, Maryland, at the same time I began to prepare to take the ECFMG exam, which is given to foreign medical students looking to transfer to medical schools in the United States.

It was the summer of 1982. I had finished up my three years in Guadalajara. I was studying hard for the ECFMG and playing hard as usual—living at home but spending a lot of weekends in New Jersey. I had a friend named Clay who pitched in with nine other young professionals who worked in New York City to rent a beach house in Long Branch, New Jersey—a common arrangement given how expensive it was to rent these prime spots on the ocean. The house had a little sign identifying it as The Chateau, so that's how we referred to it: "Let's go out to the chateau for the weekend!" Despite how many people were sharing the place, everyone was working so the number of guests in the house on the weekends could be very small.

Clay and I and several other college roommates were at the chateau for the Fourth of July weekend and we got the idea to go to a disco. We parked outside of a miniature golf course and two of our college friends, who'd had several beers, somehow got into the place and called to us in the darkness.

"Here, catch!" one said, and the next thing a 6-foot-tall, 40-pound, pink plastic flamingo came flying over the fence. It knocked me over and bounced onto the road. I laughed, and so did Clay. Then, our friends scrambled out of the locked golf course and climbed into my car so we could go out drinking at the disco. Well, the flamingo had to go somewhere, so we stuffed it into the trunk and off we went.

We had to drop off one of the fellows at the train station the next morning so he could get back to Manhattan to work. Clay and I said good-bye to him then noticed a nearby bar where we could have some "hair of the dog" to cure our hangovers. After one beer, we were feeling fine. We grabbed some dinner at Donovan's reef, one of those great beachside Jersey bars that was destroyed years later by Hurricane Sandy. We barhopped and ended up around 11:00 p.m. at Ichabod's Bar and Grill, a yuppie place that was packed with people on a hot summer night. Ichabod's was lost to Sandy too, but I'll always remember it because of what happened to me there.

I had enjoyed a Finlandia vodka martini or two and was impressing the girls by the bar with my Ms. Pacman skills, when I turned around to see two especially pretty young women watching me. I thought they might be sisters and asked them if they were. It might have sounded like a line, but I genuinely thought they looked similar. For some reason, they didn't roll their eyes and turn their back on me. They laughed and said they weren't related and were very different from each other. They were amused that I had mistaken them for sisters. We started talking and I learned that one of them, Sue, worked at Clay's company—in fact, he was her boss. How likely is that? The other one was Dale. She was living with her parents in West Deal, a wealthy area on the Jersey Shore and looking forward to her second year as a schoolteacher. She told me she was hoping to line up a job in the Princeton area in the fall. By the end of the evening, both girls had given me their phone numbers.

We left them and, at some point, Clay and I decided to return the pink flamingo to the golf course. When we arrived, it was closed. The next thing I knew, I was waking up in the chateau and thinking, *Whatever happened to that flamingo?* I got up and started walking around the place, and sure enough, I found it—planted in the backyard. Clay and I did the right thing and brought it back to its home. The miniature golf course was still closed, so we had to toss it over the fence and hope the colorful fellow would somehow find his way back home to the ninth green.

When we got back, I found the phone numbers in my pocket, and said to Clay, "Hey, do you remember that one girl, Dale? Was she as pretty as I remembered thinking she was?"

He said, "I don't know. I guess so."

The night was a bit fuzzy in my memory, but I was glad that I'd remembered her as a girl I really did want to call. I phoned her from the weekend house and we met up at the beach club in Ocean Grove on the North Jersey Shore, played some tennis, and went out to dinner at Colt's Neck near Freehold—Springsteen country. Dale and I began a relationship that continued for 24 years.

A few days after that memorable weekend, the admission committee was set to meet. So on the morning of July 20, I called the University of Maryland and spoke to their secretary to check on whether I was accepted for transfer or not. She said, "Let me look here ... Steven Heird, you have been accepted in transfer to the University of Maryland School of Medicine."

Yesssss! Was I glad I'd called! I was at my parents' house, and I ran from room to room looking for them to share my good news. They were very excited for me. And they were also very happy that the university's tuition was half of what Universidad Autónoma de Guadalajara charged.

My life's course had just changed dramatically. It was a lot to take in. Quickly, my mind started going down a list of details. I still had a furnished apartment in Mexico and I had already paid for the next semester's tuition, which was several thousand dollars. I immediately made plans to fly back to Mexico and sell my furniture to another American medical student and recover some of my tuition from the medical school in Mexico if I could (I ended up getting half of it back). Then, I would return to the United States to repeat my third year of clinical medical school at the University of Maryland. That would give me the opportunity to gain more clinical experience in various disciplines and rotations as a medical student. It also would enhance my chances of obtaining a surgical residency position after I completed my fourth year of medical school.

I began asking my medical school friends in Mexico if they knew anyone in Baltimore that might need a roommate, and someone directed me to a friend who was an insurance agent who had an apartment off of Loch Raven Boulevard in a community just north of Baltimore. I moved in with him and began dating Dale, who was now living in Ewing, New Jersey—almost a three-hour-long drive from me. Given that I'd had a four-hour commute to my girlfriend's home back when I was at Washington and Lee, a three-hour drive felt doable.

Then, I began my clinical rotations. Because I'd entered the class in the summer rather than the year before, most of the best rotations had already been snatched up by other medical students. I had really wanted several different surgery rotations, but I would just have to take what was available.

It turned out that my roommate, who worked 9 to 5, really loved to smoke pot, so in the evenings he was always smoking it, which was okay with me. I started smoking with him at the end of the day sometimes, but it didn't interfere with my ability to do the rotations. I didn't have to do drug tests, and it didn't affect my alertness. MTV had just come out and I was transfixed watching Michael Jackson turn into a monster in his "Thriller" video. When I wasn't checking out this new music video channel, I was watching sports, especially the Baltimore Colts and Baltimore Orioles, on the color television we had picked up for the apartment.

One odd thing about where I lived is that I could hear the constant banging of doors from the people across the hall, especially on a Sunday night. How many visitors could my neighbors have in a day? My roommate decided to check it out and reported back that they were drug dealers—

regular guys who were students at a local university and bought cocaine in New York City on weekends to resell out of their apartment. Their customers knew that there was always a fresh shipment on Sunday nights. "They want to meet you," my roommate said. "They can't believe a medical student does drugs."

I didn't know how to feel about that reputation but it was true, I did drugs. The next time my roommate went across the hall, I went with them to get to know my neighbors. Both were from middle class backgrounds—one of them had a father who was a judge in New York City. They were clean-cut college guys with no black light or marijuana leaf posters or bongs lying around.

Maybe they picked up on the fact that my roommate was a pothead. Maybe we just had a "we buy drugs on occasion" vibe and that's why they were so quick to admit to what they were doing and even how they were doing it. At one point, they showed me their paraphernalia to cook freebase cocaine. I said, "Isn't that dangerous? Isn't that what Richard Pryor did?" I remembered a couple years before when the comedian had been seriously burned when his freebasing cocaine caused an explosion. My neighbors said they were using a different method than he had, and explained how it was much safer. Their explanation convinced me I didn't need to worry about them turning the apartment into a pile of rubble. The word "crack" didn't exist yet, but that's what they were concocting in their still.

I tried it once, and the high was so intense it scared me. I could see how someone could become addicted to it very quickly. After that, I stuck to my drugs of choice that worked for me, namely, alcohol and marijuana. I didn't have access to Ritalin, or I probably would have used it to stay awake when drinking.

I didn't allow anything to hinder my work. To burn off stress, I jogged and played some pickup basketball. And as I said, I smoked a little pot and drank at bars on occasion. I'd meet up with Dale on the weekends and go to movies, or socialize with her friends over dinner or at bars. Alcohol wasn't the focal point of the evening, but it was a part of it much of the time. Dale enjoyed wine, while I liked my beer.

I was able to get As and Bs on all my rotations, which was great. Everything was going well, or so I thought. I didn't realize I was in for a wake-up call.

A Sobering
Wake-up Call

Chapter Fourteen

I t was a Tuesday night and I was on pediatric rotation, which was not very demanding, so when a friend named Stan asked me to go out and party with him, I said yes. I figured I could pull off a late night having fun without paying a price the next day. I picked him up, along with a friend of his named Don who wanted to tag along, at Stan's apartment in Baltimore City. We drove to Hammer Jack's, a popular hard rock bar in downtown Baltimore off of Russell Street, and drank beer and did shots of Kahlua and vodka for quite a while. I ignored my prohibition against dark liquor, because it had been a very long time since I'd had it and Don and Stan were eager to do shots. I didn't want to spoil the party, I guess.

We each did several shots and then, around 11:00 p.m., I felt tired and said I needed to go home. The three of us left Hammer Jack's, and I was extra cautious as I drove out of the city on Calvert Street, a two-lane street with a moderate amount of traffic that I was very familiar with. I could tell that I was buzzed and probably couldn't pass a Breathalyzer test if I were to be pulled over, so I didn't want to make any driving mistakes as I drove toward Johns Hopkins University.

My plan was to drop off Stan, my old friend, but he had climbed into the backseat and drifted off to sleep, and I was chatting away with Don, in the passenger seat, about his experiences as a medical student. In fact, our conversation got so involved that I went straight to Don's place and dropped him off, and then started back to my own apartment, only to suddenly realize I'd forgotten Stan, who was fast asleep in the back.

Damn! I thought. I really didn't want to double back toward his apartment. I woke him up and he shook off his grogginess.

"I'm really tired," I told him. "Do you mind staying over at my place and I'll drop you off in the morning?"

"Aw, come on. Take me home. It's only 20 minutes out of your way," he pleaded. My instincts told me to say no, but I didn't. It was easier to cave in and not disappoint my friend. I turned around and dropped him off, and then drove back up Calvert Street to get home.

I knew the lights were staggered so that if you drove 25 miles per hour going north, you wouldn't have to slow down or stop. As I pulled onto the road, I could see the lights ahead of me and decided it would be easy to catch all of them as they were green. Unfortunately, I wasn't a good judge of my speed and was going a little fast, so I started to fall out of synch with the green lights. At 26th street, I sensed my timing was off, but I was too slow-witted to figure out how to self-correct. At 27th, I realized my problem was that I had to slow down a bit, but before I knew it, I was at 28th street, a busy cross street, and I entered it before the red light turned to green. I knew I'd made a mistake and instantly looked to the left to see if anything was coming.

Crash. Thud. Then, blackness as someone hit me in the head with a two-by-four—at least, that's what it felt like.

You fucked up, I thought. The next instant, my vehicle, which was moving as a result of the impact, careened into a parked car. The seatbelt and shoulder belt held me back so I didn't hit the steering wheel with my head, but my arms flew forward and my elbows somehow slammed against it.

My car had been hit broadside on the driver's door by a van, and was now crunched up against a parked car.

I was dazed and vaguely realized I had just been in an accident. My face hurt, so I put my hands up to my forehead. It felt as if I were pressing against a warm sponge. I held my hands against my forehead and thought, *I'm bleeding. I don't want to bleed to death.* I was in shock from the trauma and still intoxicated. My sense of time was totally confused as I sat there drifting in and out of consciousness. Then, I heard a girl's voice as she started pulling at my hands, which were covering my face. "Let me see! Let me see!" she cried. I lowered my hands and she gasped, but I felt nothing.

I was only five blocks from Union Memorial Hospital, but that's not where the EMTs took me. I learned later that the lady who looked at my face was a nurse who had been walking her golden retriever along the street, and when she heard the accident and discovered how bloodied my face was, told the emergency medical crew to take me to Johns Hopkins Hospital. She knew that there, I would have access to the Wilmer Eye Institute, which is one of the premiere eye centers in the world. I believe the fact that a nurse who had knowledge of the eye center passed by just as I collided with the van is a sign that God was looking after me. I believe I needed a wake-up call, and that I was not destined to lose my eyesight or my livelihood.

I sat there in my car, dazed, until the EMT crew helped me out of it. They put me in a neck brace and guided me onto a gurney. Once in the ambulance, I could hear the siren overhead wailing. It felt as if we were just sort of bumping along, and I thought, *This thing feels like it's made of tin. Huh. Not very sophisticated.* I still hadn't processed what had just happened. I couldn't see what was happening around me, because my right eye was completely shut and my left eye was rapidly swelling up.

When I got into the ER, I told the doctors that I was fully awake and a medical student from the University of Maryland. I said, "Just let me know what you have to do before you do it. I'll cooperate." Because of my injuries, my eyes were swollen shut. A CAT scan and workup showed that my face was the only part of my body that had suffered in the accident.

After stabilizing me, they discharged me to the Wilmer Eye Institute, which was in the same facility. It turned out that I had a penny-sized, circular piece of plastic from the grill of the van wedged between my eyeball and the orbit of my right eye. My eyebrows and eyelids had vertical cuts through them as well as transverse cuts from the plastic on the grill. In fact, my face was so diced up that later, when I saw a photograph of all the injuries, I thought it looked like a Picasso cubism painting because nothing was quite lined up.

I would need surgery.

My brother came to clinic immediately upon hearing the news, and though the bandages on my eyes prevented me from seeing him, I was comforted by his presence. I was taking the bare minimum of pain medications. My mouth was extremely dry because I was dehydrated, but I wouldn't be allowed to drink until after surgery the next day. Rusty told me my parents were on their way, having cut short their ski vacation in Vermont as soon as they heard the news about me. They probably wouldn't make it down before I was wheeled into surgery the next morning.

I met my surgeon and quickly developed faith in him. When he told me I might lose my right eye, I was determined to be positive—and to pray.

The last thing I recall before surgery is being rolled into the OR and a female anesthesiologist telling me to breathe. Apparently, she had given me the anesthesia already, but she knew that my breathing consciously and slowly would relax me so that I would succumb to the medicine more quickly, and lose consciousness. I said, "Ma'am, I'm unable to breathe. You need to start breathing for me." I'm sure she had heard many incoherent statements from patients who are disoriented and woozy, and she knew there was no point in trying to reason with me in my confused state.

Next thing I knew, I woke up in the recovery room and my mother's voice called my name. She must have been very scared because she hadn't yet heard whether they'd been able to save my eye. I was too out of it to ask her if that was the case. But within hours, my surgeon came in and gave me the good news that both my eyes were intact and my sight might return.

After a day or so, my surgeon came in to take my bandages off my left eye, which was the least injured. Once it was uncovered, I could see light through the swollen tissue. This gave me hope, and I tried hard not to think about the possibility that I would lose my right eye, or at least sight in it. It was very hard not to worry, though. I thought, *All this hard work, for so many years—what if you've blown it? Who is going to let a one-eyed surgeon work on him?* I knew I had no control over my recovery and had to put faith in my surgeon and God. It was out of my hands and I couldn't bear to think about what my life would be like if I didn't regain my sight completely.

The next day, I was sitting in my hospital bed when I heard and felt someone come in. I didn't know who it was but I had a deep sense that this was an important person who was much admired, someone who would help me. My surgeon called my name and I realized it was him and his team of medical students who were there to observe.

Slowly, he peeled off the bandage and light flooded into my right eye. "Looking better," he said. He said something to his cadre of students but I didn't take in what it was. All I could think about was that I might get my sight back.

My surgeon left and I experienced an incredible adrenaline rush. In fact, I was so hyper and exhilarated I felt I had to call the nurse to make sure I was okay. My heart was beating like a hummingbird's wings.

As it sunk in that I really was recovering nicely, I felt a rush of gratitude toward the doctors and nurses and to God. In those few days after surgery, I had beaten myself up plenty, thinking, *Now I'll never be a surgeon. How stupid!* I had been drinking and I think I smoked a little pot. Were those actions bigger factors in the accident than being tired and speeding were?

A few days later, the doctor took the patch off my right eye, and through the swollen tissue, I was actually able to see light out of my right eye also. I was told these were good signs, and within a couple of days I was discharged with the promise that when the swelling went down, my vision would return to both eyes. Fortunately, the doctors were right about that.

At this point, I told myself, "I think I have a drinking problem." I'd had a psychiatric rotation already and the professor had been very insistent that if you have a DUI, you are an alcoholic. I didn't know there was a list of questions that are commonly used to determine whether a person has a drinking problem. I just knew what my professor had taught me. I thought, *I need to look into this.* Had my blood alcohol been high enough to qualify me for a DUI? I had no idea what my levels were. Apparently, the police officer at the scene of my accident had come to the emergency room suspecting that I was intoxicated and had asked for me to sign for a blood alcohol level, which was routine at that time in 1983. However, the emergency room physicians told him he could not come in because I was too badly injured. He never returned to try to issue a DUI citation or to check up on things—too busy, I guess. Still, I knew they had done an alcohol blood level with the trauma panel when I first came into the emergency room. And while neither my car insurance company nor my health insurance company cared to follow up, the question of whether I had an illegal blood alcohol count bothered me. The thought in the back of my mind was that if the police officer came to give me a citation for DUI and the blood alcohol level was available for me to check, maybe I should check it. If I was legally drunk, then maybe I was an alcoholic after all.

I decided to go to the medical records department of Johns Hopkins University and ask for my records to see just how intoxicated I was. When the records clerk told me I'd have to pay ten dollars to get a copy, I decided it wasn't that important for me to know whether or not I was an alcoholic, so I walked away. It didn't seem to be worth $10 for me to know something that I now know was a critical piece of information, but that's alcoholic thinking for you. That tiny obstacle to learning the truth gave me a good excuse to remain in denial.

I was able to admit to myself that I felt I was going too quickly through life and needed to slow down. I was in a lot of physical pain after the accident and it took me six weeks to get back to normal activities. I realized I'd almost killed myself, and I was fortunate not to have lost my eyesight. Now, I know that alcohol was a major contributing factor to the accident, but at the time I resisted taking a hard look at my drinking. I had been drinking Kahlua, a dark liquor, so I went back to the old rationalization that my problem wasn't drinking but drinking dark alcohol.

I also rationalized that I just needed to slow down. Several of my friends were getting married, and maybe it was time for me to do that, too. If I got married, I reasoned, I would stop making immature decisions, like drinking and driving when I was tired. I would be committing to a new way of life.

Dale had a job. She was pretty, smart, and sociable. I liked her a lot. And she came to my aid when my mom told her about the car accident. I told myself, *If I marry her, I'll settle down and I won't be in danger of killing myself again.* Much later, in rehab, I would be able to see that my reasoning in marrying her was part of an addictive thinking pattern. It's not up to anyone else to keep you from drinking. A person's drinking behaviors and habits are his own responsibility. I didn't expect Dale to take drinks out of my hand, but I did expect that she would be a calming influence, so much so that my drinking habits would naturally be tempered to the point where I wouldn't get into trouble or danger anymore.

I bought an engagement ring, and then contacted Dale's father to let him know that I was intending to ask his daughter for her hand. He gave my plan his blessing. Then, I made reservations for Dale and me to have dinner at the nice restaurant on the 13th floor of the Hyatt in Baltimore's Inner Harbor. I asked her to marry me that night at the end of our meal, and she accepted. It was an ideal engagement evening. I was looking forward to a safe, happy future as a married man and medical resident.

Beginning Residency and Married Life

Chapter Fifteen

I was at the University of Maryland in Baltimore, still in the clinical portion of medical school. I had chosen some surgery rotations as part of my medical school education: cardiovascular, oncology, and vascular. I was still wearing the short white jacket that signals to patients that you're not ready for the long coat—there is still much to learn.

I had already worked for an entire year at various hospitals, including the busy Bronx Lebanon in New York. For that one, I stayed with the parents of my boxer roommate Jimmy, but as with most rotations, it only lasted about six weeks and I was on to the next one. But for that short while, I enjoyed driving in from Teaneck, NJ, over the GW Bridge to the Bronx, and chuckling at the antics of a rising star among the morning talk radio shows—Howard Stern. Most of the other rotations were in the Baltimore area, so I was able to live with my parents and commute to the various hospitals.

For every physician, whatever their specialty, the first time a patient dies, it sears an impression on your mind. The patient that initiated me into the experience of having to accept my helplessness in the face of a patient's death was a woman I'll call Elizabeth.

She was an attractive woman in her late thirties, slender, with long dark hair. She came in with her husband and told us she had two daughters, ten and twelve years old. Elizabeth had been battling leukemia for five years and during chemo, it was discovered she had a dangerously low level of platelets in her blood—these are the cells that form blood clots, which prevent a person from bleeding to death. But her immediate complaint was shortness of breath. Our job was to get her platelets so she couldn't accidentally bleed out if, for example, she had a stroke. Elizabeth was admitted, and a doctor, learning of her shortness of breath but not checking her chart carefully, decided to have a blood sample drawn to check her blood oxygen levels. Nowadays, she'd be in the ER with a little plastic clip on her finger to measure these levels, but at the time, the way to get an accurate figure was to do a blood draw—meaning that a staff member would have to break her skin.

Can you see where this is going? The needle went into Elizabeth's skin in the crook of her elbow and she began to bleed. The blood started to seep into her tissues and her arm began to blow up like a balloon. They called in the vascular surgeons to stop the bleeding.

By this point in my residency, I had chosen to specialize in vascular surgery. The hole in Elizabeth's skin was tiny, of course, but the hematoma on her skin was rapidly expanding. If we didn't stop the bleeding, she would lose her arm—but if we amputated it, we would have the same challenge of trying to stop uncontrolled bleeding in a woman who had almost no platelets to clot her blood.

As a medical student, I assisted the surgeon as he tried to quickly contain the bleeding while platelets were transfused in the hope that the blood would begin to clot. We wiped up blood, and the surgeon began to stitch up the artery. He was able to complete the surgery, but her blood was running out of her like water now that we had a bigger hole in her skin where we'd made the surgical cut. We tried to use a drain but could see that she was still in danger of losing her arm and possibly bleeding to death.

We temporarily left Elizabeth and her husband to have some privacy. They spoke together quietly. When we regrouped, she told us she had decided it was time to stop fighting the leukemia. That meant she would bleed to death, maybe within a day or so.

I was shocked. How could she not fight when she had young daughters, and there was still some hope of keeping her alive? She was going to let a stupid medical error take her down? I didn't have the answer to what to do except to get creative and trying to figure out all our options and which would be the best one. And now she was cutting us off and saying, "Stop." Never having been in a situation like hers, I couldn't comprehend it. I hated feeling powerless, and I was furious at the doctor who had ordered the test without checking every detail of her chart for contraindications. While I clenched my jaw, Elizabeth's family came into her room and surrounded her bed. Their vigil continued into the night, and she slipped away peacefully. She wasn't actually my patient, but she was a patient whose team I was a part of and it was hard for me to accept her decision to receive no more help from us. In time, with more experience, I would come to understand why she'd gracefully accepted her fate, but I was still young, green, and eager, and very upset that I couldn't fix her situation.

I continued with surgery rotations—and I enjoyed them, even though the work was incredibly challenging. Sometimes, like all medical students, I'd have to be prepared to stay up for 36 hours at a stretch. Fortunately, I usually got to catch some sleep when the hospital was quiet. I became a master of sleeping when it was convenient to do so. Often, a nurse would wake me up to do a fever workup, which meant shaking off the sleep, going in to the supply room to pick up what I needed, and then walking quietly into a patient's room, where you would softly inform him or her that you were going to do a blood draw. Afterward, you would take the vials of blood to the lab, fill out paperwork, and hope you did everything right so they didn't wake you up again to repeat the process. Or I would get woken up to start IVs. This is what we called the "scut work" of residency, but it was important to do it right.

One night, a patient suspected of having TB needed a fever workup. He was an elderly African American man, and seemed to be sound asleep as I walked in on autopilot, put my supplies on his bedside table, then walked out to fetch an item I had forgotten. I returned, put a tourniquet on his arm, turned on a light to see better—and realized he was dead. Well, that woke me up completely. I called in an arrest alarm, pronto, which meant the nurse announced a code over the intercom and doctors and nurses hurried into the room. They did CPR on him, but didn't revive him. That was the first patient to die on my watch.

As the long nights and days of dealing with the mundane details and life-and-death situations continued, more than ever, I felt the need to reward myself by playing hard. One Thursday night, a resident on the medical service invited the medical students to the local watering hole the residents regularly went to after work. I got a nice beer buzz going and laughed with some fellow students while we talked shop and the jukebox played the Police and Michael Jackson. We were laughing about the experiences of the day, the challenges we faced with the various patients, the mistakes that we'd made, and the good decisions we took pride in. On those nights, I felt a sense of euphoria that I tried to recapture in the days that followed.

I started to go back to the same bar after work again and again to see if there were any other medical students or residents there. If there were, I would hang out with them. And if there weren't, I would have a few beers myself and play video games, which I found relaxing. It might have made more sense to just go home and study, but I liked that feeling of the release from the day with a couple beers. That buzzed feeling was my reward for my work, and it became very attractive to me. As long as it wasn't interfering with my goals and my life, I was going to experience it whenever I could fit it in.

There was a pattern of the intensity of my work that Dale would have to become accustomed as the fiancée and, later, wife of a surgical resident. The intensity wouldn't let up for about five years, I warned her. She said she could deal with the crazy schedule, but in retrospect, I don't think she quite had a grasp of how challenging it could be for her. She would also have to deal with the uncertainty of not knowing where I would end up working—or doing residencies in the meanwhile.

On May 25, 1984, I was very grateful to have realized my dream of graduating from medical school, and was looking forward to starting in a general surgical residency program in York Hospital in York, Pennsylvania. I was especially grateful to my mom and dad. They really didn't understand all of the specifics of what I had to do to reach my goal, but they had always trusted my judgment and supported me emotionally and financially. I wrote them a short letter to thank them for all they had done, and signed it Steven Heird, MD. I had the letter made into a plaque that I presented to them on graduation day. It read:

Dear Mom and Dad,

A dream has come true for me today. Believe me when I say I had my doubts, but there is no doubt now. We made it! When I say "we," what I mean is everyone who has given me encouragement and support in all of its varied forms over the years. This includes instructors, friends and relatives, but most importantly, both of you. I am certain you had your doubts too. But through the long struggle, I have never received a discouraging word or doubt from you, just genuine support and encouragement. That has made all the difference. I could not have made it without you. Mom and Dad, I want you to know that all of your love and support over the many years will never be forgotten. Thank you for everything.

Your son,
Steven Buchman Heird, M.D.

I got the idea from having won the Maryland Scholar Athlete award that came with an inscribed plaque that meant a lot to me. I wanted to give my parents more than just the letter—and put my expression of gratitude in a more permanent form than pen-on-paper. When I picked it up and looked at it the first time, I thought about how I had been a kid with a simple life on a farm, who used to step in turkey manure with his bare feet and wash it off in a puddle. I thought about my parents not having spent even one day in college. I thought about how I'd had to teach myself how to study to get around my learning challenges, and gone all the way to Mexico and back to achieve my dream of becoming a doctor. The arc of my journey was humbling.

And now, I was facing life as an MD and groom-to-be. My wedding was set for a month later. I didn't want to fall behind in my work, so I put off a honeymoon indefinitely. I just hadn't felt comfortable pushing my professors to let me take the time off. In part, that's because I was doing a rotation on vascular surgery, which was a very busy rotation—and York Hospital was a very busy hospital. Meanwhile, I had four weeks off before the big day.

I enjoyed helping Dale plan the wedding while she finished the school year teaching. I also started learning to play golf, which I was just terrible at, but wanted to master someday. I figured now was a good time to start, since I wouldn't have a long break again for many years.

Both of us were glad that I had solidified a residency at York Hospital, which would last for five years. I would be near my family, and Dale would have the stability of knowing where we would be living—or so we thought.

I filled out my paperwork and got my Pennsylvania medical license, and then we bought a bedroom set and procured a secondhand couch—since we really didn't have a lot of money for new furniture. Then, in June, I did two days of orientation on a Thursday and Friday before heading off for the rehearsal dinner.

The next day, Dale and I got married and held a reception. Sunday morning, after an elegant breakfast at the hotel where we'd spent our wedding night, we drove the four hours back to York, opened our wedding gifts and got a little rest. Then, on Monday morning, I started my residency program.

I left my bride alone in a new town and in a new apartment until Tuesday evening at 8:00 p.m. when I finished my first night on call and my first 36-hour day. Dale had fixed a nice first meal for us—beef stroganoff, which I'd always loved as a kid. I kept calling her and telling her I was coming home soon, but then I'd get assigned another task to complete before I could leave. By the time I walked through the door, the stroganoff had been warmed up about three times. Still, she wasn't angry at me. She knew what she was getting into, so what could she do but shrug it off?

Dale would be working as a teacher again in the fall, and my internship, of course, was work, work, work. Recognizing I was going to be in York for five years, we decided to buy a house, which we did the following June. We found a three-bedroom, two-story brick that was ready for us to move in immediately. It was perfect. I imagine for Dale, the dream life of a doctor's wife and a cute house in the suburbs had begun, even though the schedule of a resident is much more grueling than that of a surgeon. We weren't "there" yet—and the kids we planned to have were a few years off—but buying the house definitely made it feel as if we'd started a new chapter.

But after living in the house for several weeks, we started thinking about how we could upgrade it. At first, it was just a few things, like covering some brightly colored walls with neutral wallpaper. We couldn't afford a high quality wallpaper hanger, so we hired the wife of a friend who, we soon realized, didn't really know what she was doing. I thought, *You know, I could do this myself.* Having grown up on a farm, I had some handyman skills. It didn't seem like all that big a project to fit in to our busy schedule. Easy enough, right?

But the futzing with the house didn't stop at that. Once we saw how good the walls looked in that room, we decided to do something about the walls in another room. Then, once I had repainted or wallpapered those, we would find ourselves sitting in yet another room and thinking, *You know… we could do this room, too.* And so it went until we had redone every room in the house and finished the basement. I enjoyed the challenge, and Dale enjoyed coming up with ideas for what I could do next.

My parents' home was simple, so I hadn't realized how much work a house can be, or how much money it can suck up. At one point early on, Dale told me we needed to get some "window treatments" for the formal dining room. "You mean curtains?" I asked. I didn't realize the difference between the two. Apparently, it's about $1,500 a set. But Dale insisted that in a formal dining room, you had to have "window treatments."

Despite all the home renovations and 36-hour shifts, I still found some time to myself. I liked to jog. Often, I would come home from the hospital exhausted and flop on the bed only to have my dog, Brandy, a Sheltie, bark at me happily and spin around in circles, trying to get me to take her outside. She loved to jog with me, and tired though I was, I almost always pulled myself off the bed, changed, and got out there on the streets with her to do a five-mile jog. When I got home, I felt energized.

Months went by, Dale and I celebrated Christmas together in our new home for the first time, and then, one Sunday morning in the second year of my surgical residency, I had an unsettling and disturbing experience. The on-call trauma surgeon was a fourth year surgical resident and my job was to assist him. I had to assess any trauma cases that came in and make sure we had plenty of blood ready to go if surgery was needed, put in an IV if it was needed, take patient histories—the small stuff that's important to do right. There had been a Halloween party the night before, and I was hung-over and not feeling very good. I knew I had to push through it and I figured I could sleep off the effects later, after my shift was over.

Then, a ten-year-old boy came into the emergency room to get treated for a stab wound caused by a hunting knife he'd received as a birthday gift from his grandmother. The boy had been riding around on his bicycle showing off his new knife to his friends. Then, while holding the knife, he popped a wheelie, lost control of the bike, fell off, and accidentally stabbed himself in the left shoulder. He came into the emergency room pale with a weak pulse, but awake.

We took a chest X-ray and the left side of his chest looked cloudy, indicating that the area was filling up with blood. Immediately, he was wheeled into the operating room where a heart surgeon and the surgical resident trauma surgeon would operate on him. Although the boy had come to the ER immediately, he was bleeding so severely that he went into cardiac arrest and died on the operating table. As I watched helplessly, I couldn't believe it. How could we lose a healthy kid to such a stupid accident when we were doing our best as a team? As the heart surgeon called the time of death, I stared at his lifeless body, my mind reeling.

Later, when reviewing the case, we discovered that he had two holes, not one, in the superior vena cava, the main vein in the chest—talk about a freak accident! If we had known about the second hole, which was hidden from sight, the vascular surgeon could have sewn it up—and probably saved his life. I had chosen vascular surgery because of its life-or-death aspects, and this experience solidified my decision to go into that specialty. It also made me vow never again to drink and allow myself to be hung-over and under the weather when I was on call. My less-than-sparkling condition hadn't been a factor in this boy's death, but what would happen next time? I wasn't going to take any chances. I was better than that.

Chapter Sixteen

Birth and Death

I t was a Friday night in 1987, four years into my training, and I was the trauma surgeon on call. I had fallen asleep at 7:30 p.m., anticipating a long night. The weekends always brought drinking and driving and bad car accidents, and since it was just a few days before Christmas, the number of inebriated drivers on the road would be increased by the holiday revelry. Dale was home pregnant with our son Billy, who was due after the first of the year. She wasn't expecting me home until morning.

At 11:30 p.m., I woke up from my nap in a darkened room of the hospital feeling ready to go. I put my shoes on, walked down the hall to use to the restroom before going back on duty, stretched, and thought, *I'm so fresh, I wouldn't even mind if a trauma patient came in right now.* As soon as the thought formed in my head, the cardiac arrest alarm on the monitors began buzzing. I looked up at the screen and saw 4SW, a post-labor recovery ward. That was unusual. I knew some woman must have had complications during or after giving birth.

Although I didn't have to show up for a cardiac arrest in the hospital, only for trauma patients in the emergency room, I made the decision to go to the labor and delivery floor to see if I could help. I jogged up the three flights of stairs and at the door out of the stairwell, I ran into a resident who had come from another floor. Together, we went on to the floor and looked for the room that had the medical emergency.

She was a thin, pretty young woman with long, dark blonde hair, and her big belly was pushing against the hospital gown she wore. She was clearly unresponsive, and lying in the arms of a man whose face was nearly white with fear, who seemed to be her husband. As diplomatically as possible, a nurse directed him to a waiting room down the hall as another resident and nurse filled us in on the details. The other resident and I began to put her on a backboard to intubate her and start chest compressions. Apparently, she had a melanoma in her lungs and decided not to get treatment, which would have harmed the baby. We learned she was very religious, and was putting her fate in God's hands as she continued the pregnancy.

Kathy, the OB (obstetric) resident arrived, and someone got an IV in the mother and continued chest compressions. I stepped back to observe and be on alert should they need me for anything. I listened to the OB intern rapidly rattle off facts about the condition of the patient and the unborn baby. The patient had come in with contractions despite being only 23 weeks along in her pregnancy, and the contractions had been stopped successfully—but then, the mother stopped breathing. We were going to have to perform an emergency C-section to ensure the baby would live. The OB said the mother was on steroids because the cancer was making it difficult for her to breathe. That was good news for the baby, since steroids can speed up the development of a premature baby's lungs, which would give the baby a better chance of survival once he or she was out of the womb.

I knew the mother's condition was terminal, but we hoped she would survive to meet her baby. The doctors had hoped to discharge her in the morning so she could continue the pregnancy to term, but now, that plan didn't seem realistic.

I continued to stand in the back of the room as the events unfolded before me. As the seconds and minutes ticked away, she did not respond to the resuscitation. Her heart still wasn't beating—I suspected she'd had a massive pulmonary embolism. It was too hectic to even get a fetal monitor on her, but we all knew that every second the baby remained in her meant less of a chance of it being born alive.

Then, I heard a male voice say to me, the only surgical resident in the room, "If anyone is going to do anything, it's going to have to be you." It was a clear call to action. Calmly, I said to Kathy, "You need to get the baby out."

Without responding, she hurried out to get ready in the labor and delivery operating room. I'm sure she had the same thought I had in that moment.

I had training to draw on. I was alert and focused. I said to no one in particular, "We need to call a neonatologist"—a specialist in treating babies.

A hand went up in the back of the room. "I'm here."

I spun around. "Call the OB resident back and give me a number 12 scalpel blade," I said, recognizing if I asked for a handle for the blade as well, it would cause a delay. Moments later, holding just the blade, I cut into the belly of the lifeless young woman. I wasn't wearing gloves, and accidentally cut myself as her belly rose up and down in response to the chest compressions. Kathy arrived just as I cut open the uterus. There was a gush of blood.

Kathy put her hand into the womb and pulled out a bloody, wet, baby boy. As she cradled him, I pinched the umbilical cord and cut it. We immediately handed him over to the neonatologist, who then rushed out the door to meet with a nurse who was hurriedly wheeling an incubator toward him.

The baby was tiny, but he was breathing. I stopped for a moment and looked over at the body of the mother. The time of death was called, and the light in the room cast an eerie glow—or maybe it just seemed that way, as I realized that this young mother, who had so desperately wanted to give birth to her baby that she had sacrificed her own life, was truly gone.

I glanced into the hall and saw the neonatologist and nurse pushing the incubator toward the NICU, or neonatal intensive care unit. We were done. For a moment, I just stood there with bloody hands.

"What now?" someone said.

I looked at the gaping hole in the young mother's abdomen. "Pack the wounds," I said. It was futile, but it seemed the right thing to do, out of respect.

I washed my hands, found the cut and doused it with alcohol, and then bandaged it. The fear of HIV infection was far from my mind. I knew that being a surgeon, I would always be at risk of accidentally exchanging fluids with a patient. I couldn't even think about that at a moment such as this.

Minutes later, I found myself walking quietly down the stairs to the floor where the hospital chapel was located, as if pulled there by an unseen force. It was a small room with polished wooden benches and soft, yellow lighting. I took a seat and faced the podium that served as an altar. And I began to reflect.

Everything I had worked for or done had brought me to this moment. I thought about Dale back home, sleeping soundly, my own son inside her womb, preparing to be ushered into our arms in just a few weeks. I was overwhelmed with humility and gratitude.

As I sat there, taking in what had just happened, a thought returned: Whose voice had spoken to me, telling me it was up to me to do something? In that instant, I realized it hadn't come from anyone in the room. Was it the voice of God, telling me to take charge of the situation and move quickly? Or was it my conscience?

I felt an inner knowing that the voice was divinely inspired. I was meant to save that baby's life. This is why I had done all the hard work I'd had, why I'd had to struggle with doubts about myself and whether I really could reach my goal of being a doctor. This was the reason for everything—one fragile life.

A few weeks after that emotional night, my first child, Billy, was born on a cold, snowy January day—the very day he was due. As he emerged into the hands of the ob/gyn doing the delivery, I saw my son's red hair—red like my brother Rusty's, and like mine, which I was already starting to lose. I got so excited. This was really my son!

I felt gratitude and humility wash over me again as I held him in my arms for the first time. Saving someone else's son had provided a brief glimpse into how precious a moment this was. Life—what a miracle it is!

The Christmas baby lived and went home with his father that spring. The happy ending is that his father married one of the NICU nurses who took care of the baby from day one, so that little boy had a mother after all. I think his own mother, who made the ultimate sacrifice so that he could live, would have wanted that for him.

As for my own life, what's the saying? "And baby makes three." We had a little family now, as well as the perfect house to raise our son in. But there was just a small problem with our nest—it was in the wrong place.

When I was in my fourth year as a surgical resident, I had decided to pursue a vascular surgery fellowship and interviewed at multiple locations around the country from the University of Iowa, to Tulane University and Ochsner Clinic, both in Louisiana, to the University of Chicago, and more. And when skiing that year, I met a vascular surgeon who worked at McGill University who encouraged me to try to attain a two-year vascular surgery fellowship at McGill Hospital in Montreal, Canada. I explained that my plan was to use the match program to find a spot, since it matches new physicians with programs around the country that are an excellent fit for their interests and skills. I told him that if I didn't get a match, applying at McGill would be my plan B. As luck would have it, I didn't match any of the 45 programs that were available in the United States. Now, I needed to get the McGill fellowship—but that would mean a move to Canada.

The physician at McGill was sure the NIH grant they had applied for would go through and my fellowship would be paid. I explained this to Dale, who said, "But there's no guarantee, right?" True, but I figured I would deal with the money issue when I came right smack up against it. For now, I had to have faith that the money would come through after all. Maybe I could get a job working in an ER in Montreal when I wasn't working at McGill. I already had been invited by Apple Hill Surgical

Associates in York to join them as a partner, starting in two years—maybe they would agree to front me some money to live on until then. There had to be a way to make it work.

I also filled out an application for the University of Pennsylvania Hospital's fellowship for a vascular surgical residency. It's one of the best in the country, so I knew there would be a lot of competition for it, but hey, as the lottery slogan goes, "If you don't play, you can't win." Very quickly, I got a letter from them saying that someone else had gotten it.

Dale was understandably nervous. Were we going to have to go to Canada, rent out our house, and scramble for money? Would I have to bide my time until fellowships opened up again in the fall?

Then, luck suddenly decided to flow my way—or maybe I attracted this opportunity. Considering how fortunate it is, I'd like to think that my positive attitude and willingness to be open to however the universe chose to open up a path for me played a role in what happened next. The newly minted doctor who had taken the University of Pennsylvania Hospital fellowship backed out. I was called; I interviewed for the fellowship—and got the news that they wanted me.

So I would have an income for the year of the fellowship after all. We would remain in Pennsylvania. But our house wasn't close enough to my workplace, and we would have to find an apartment in or near Philadelphia.

Billy was a year old, Dale was pregnant again, and she was not keen on moving. In fact, she cried a lot when we had to sublease our house, pack up our belongings and put some in storage, and move to an apartment, which was in Bryn Mawr. We even had to farm out Brandy to my parents because our apartment lease didn't allow us to have pets.

But Dale made friends in our new neighborhood and got a lot of emotional support from the women she met. She was relieved that we had an income, even if it wasn't a lot of money. And the light at the end of the tunnel was coming closer in two ways: I was graduating in June. Once I passed the American College of Surgeons National Board Exam and the tests to be certified in general and vascular surgery, I would be ready to practice surgery. And our second child was due after the end of the year.

I hoped to be inducted into the American College of Surgeons as a fellow, because it's the most prestigious surgery organization in the United States. To get that FACS after my name would be an incredible honor that would require extra work and extra examinations, including oral exams, but I really wanted it, so that was in my plan. Dale couldn't understand why I wasn't willing to just be a general surgeon with no frills. She was impatient and wanted to get settled, and we had to take that extra year in the Philadelphia area—and now I wanted to take more exams.

Dale and I went to tour the labor and delivery floor of the hospital where she was going to give birth to Jonathan. They were slated for a renovation the next spring, but Dale was due in January, and the dingy tile, old furniture, and harsh lighting on the floor brought tears to her eyes. "I can't have my baby here!" she said.

I phoned our babysitter back home and asked, "Can you stay a little longer?" I wanted to have Dale tour another hospital right away. I drove her to Lankenau Hospital a few miles away, which turned out to be infinitely brighter and more welcoming. They even offered a surf and turf meal for new moms and dads for dinner after the baby was delivered. Comforted by the thought that she would have a lovely birth experience here, Dale relaxed and said she felt she would be able to find a good ob/gyn to deliver Jonathan. We'd chosen the name after the ultrasound revealed his sex— accidentally. We'd said we didn't want to know the gender, but then the ultrasound technician who was reading the screen said, "Are you sure you don't want to know?" Well, Dale and I understood immediately what that mean—the technician had seen a penis and was eager to fill us in on the news. Our big surprise was spoiled.

But of course, we got over that quickly. Like his brother, Jonathan arrived on a cold January day. I joked with the hospital staff that despite the hoopla about another mom on the floor, a local newscaster who gave birth to twins the same day Jonathan was born, my baby was the real star.

I kept up with the demanding fellowship program and gave up weekend drinking, but had a beer or two or a gin and tonic after work on many of the days when I knew I would have the evening off. I continued to jog two to five miles a day, and of course, having two babies in diapers kept me busy, too. However, Dale and I did have a chance to get away for a few days in early 1990 to a weekend event at the Dorado Country Club and Resort in Miami sponsored by a drug company. The guest speaker was the famous heart surgeon Denton Cooley, and I was really looking forward to hearing what he had to say. There would also be golfing out on the course called the green monster, which was infamous among serious golfers. My golf game had much improved by then, although I think I was kidding myself that I was on par with the other fellows who would be attending. Dale and I left Billy with his grandparents, who also had Brandy in their "foster care" until my fellowship was over. We also took Jonathan who, at three months old, was sleeping a lot and breastfeeding, so he was a pretty mobile package.

The Friday night reception was held outdoors, and we putted fluorescent golf balls on the putting greens beside the pool. They also had an open bar, which I couldn't resist given how little drinking I'd been doing. I had a gin and tonic in hand when I bumped into Denton Cooley and talked to him for a couple of minutes. It was a euphoric feeling, one I had missed. But having been away from alcohol for so long, I ended up drinking too much that night. I woke up in the hotel room hours after midnight and stumbled around trying to locate the bathroom. I began to urinate and a light came on, and then Dale said, "What are you doing? Are you … are you peeing in the closet?"

I was too drunk to be embarrassed and I made a point of brushing it aside the next day. Dale said nothing. I'm sure she was confused and embarrassed for me. It was easier for both of us to forget the incident and get back to our busy lives.

Chapter Seventeen

Buildup to a
Breaking Point

I n August, 1990, about six months after the Florida trip, I joined
what I considered the most prestigious general vascular surgery
practice in York, Pennsylvania. It was a regional trauma center, and
the vascular practice included four board-certified general surgeons. One
of them, like me, was board certified in vascular surgery as well. With
double certification, I would be practicing general surgery as well as
vascular surgery and building up the vascular surgery practice. The career
I'd been working toward my whole life was finally coming together.

But it came at the price of being at work or on call most of the time.
Because we only had two surgeons who could share the vascular surgery
duties, I had to be on call on Tuesdays, Thursdays, and on every other
weekend, I was on call Friday, Saturday, and Sunday. Every day, I had to
make rounds to see patients. And there was never a day without a call,
whether it was someone who was having trouble with their prescription
painkillers, or someone who had developed a new symptom. I often had
to have them meet me at the ER to see if the situation was serious enough

to require immediate attention or whether it could wait until the next office visit. The local emergency rooms would also call us whenever they had someone with a circulation problem who needed a vascular surgeon consult. The hospitals would call if one of our surgery patients seemed to experiencing complications, too. There was another vascular surgeon in the area, but our practice was much busier. When he was on vacation, we got every emergency call for a vascular surgeon.

The operation I liked to perform most was correcting a ruptured abdominal aortic aneurysm—a break in a blood vessel that causes internal bleeding. The condition is common in older people, typically cigarette smokers, who will often show up in the ER with low blood pressure and severe abdominal and back pain from blood pouring from the artery into the area around the kidneys. If the break isn't repaired, the person is guaranteed to die within hours. We only got about three to four of these emergencies a month, but knowing the call could come at any time kept me from traveling too far from the hospital, and my pager was pretty much glued to me. I prided myself on being able to get patients in this fragile condition of a ruptured artery off the table alive. However, the stress of the surgery on top of hardening arteries and other comorbid conditions sometimes would kill them even if they made it through the operation. I couldn't address that, but I could be the superhero who dropped everything to fly to the hospital and save a patient's life.

I also performed somewhat less urgent surgeries, which had to be done within 24 hours. Patients with blood clots, who typically had poor circulation, often due to smoking or diabetes or both, would have arteries go bad and need a bypass around the blockage. The surgeries can take up to four hours, so I had to be alert and ready to focus for a long stretch when I got to the operating room.

In addition to being on call and doing scheduled surgeries, I was busy with an expanding family. Dale and I now had two boys at home, our Sheltie, Brandy, two cars, and a house to take care of—and we had decided to build a new house now that the old one was feeling too small. It seemed we had a perfect life and that finally—after all the years of studying and preparing and moving around—I might start to feel settled. But the old feeling that there had to be something more to life tugged at me. I never seemed to be doing enough. There was a dissatisfaction and yearning within me that I couldn't explain to myself, much less articulate to Dale. Life became about doing what was on the agenda, working hard, and playing hard. I was enslaved by my calendar and my "To Do" list.

My drinking was confined to a gin and tonic or beer or two after work. I certainly never lost control or got drunk as I had in college. Consequently, the thought that I might be developing a problem with alcohol never occurred to me. Alcoholism can be insidious—it was for me.

Dale enjoyed wine, and we'd often split a bottle over dinner. The first glass hit the spot for me, but for some reason, as time went on, I started pouring another and another. Afterward, I would think, *I didn't really need those other glasses. Why didn't I stop at one?* There never seemed to be an answer, but then, I didn't look too hard for one either. My drinking wasn't regular, and it didn't interfere with my work or being on call. And I didn't get hangovers.

I continued to be physically active, which helped me maintain my energy level. My wife loved tennis, and playing it together was a big part of our lives before and after we got married. Being a competitive, athletic guy, I had fun playing with her. We joined a club and got in plenty of doubles, partners, and singles games with friends and other club members.

In the early summer in 1994, our third son, Andrew, was born. By then, I was well into the swing of being a surgeon and a dad. Billy was playing T-ball and it was clear he was a gifted athlete. I'd been playing catch with him since he turned three, using a Velcro glove and ball, and noticed he could catch the ball even when I threw it at him with force. I wanted to be the dad at every T-ball game, which seemed to be the suburban norm, unlike when I was a kid. But work kept pulling me away. My desire to see my kids play every game whenever I could set the course for years to come as each of my children took up one or even two sports. That goal became increasingly difficult to reach as my family, the number of sports, and the number of games expanded. At one point in the 2000s, Jonathan was playing basketball on two different teams, the local intramural team and his Catholic school's team. I'd race from one county to another in one day to fit in both his games on top of my scheduled surgeries and whatever else was going on. The madness of suburban family sports activities and the demands they impose crept up on me. Everyone around me seemed to be chasing here and there in an SUV as well, and I didn't stop to think, *This is too much.*

But back to 1994, the year Andrew was born. The busyness of family life didn't quite seem so crazy back then, and I felt on top of things with my pager, portable phone, calm temper, and ability to prioritize. One hot Friday afternoon, after I completed rounds to see my patients in the hospital, a job I didn't like to delegate to a partner, I went to the local pool to meet my wife and the boys and her friend's son, six-year-old Russell. I guess by then I had proven my ability to multitask, because as soon as Dale saw me, she asked me to watch the baby and the older boys so she could go off and do some shopping. I was on call and would have to stay close by my pager, but I said yes anyway.

I had parked the baby, myself, and all our gear at the short end of the L-shaped pool, where there was a kiddie pool with a slide, and placed the big, thick, portable telephone I carried with me on the ground next to my pager and all our flip-flops. Russell patted me on the leg, saying, "Mr. Heird! Mr. Heird! Mr. Heird?"

"Yeah, what is it, Russell?" I answered.

"Can we go to the diving board?"

"Can you swim?"

"Oh yeah! I just learned!"

Jonathan, who was four, and Bill, now six, were both good swimmers so I gave Russell the okay, but chose to leave all our stuff rather than try to drag it all to the other end of the pool. I hoisted Andrew onto my hip and walked to the end of the pool behind the happy, bouncing boys, and then nodded and smiled as Billy jumped off the diving board. He dog paddled toward the ladder and Russell followed him. Just as Russell was about the reach the ladder, my pager went off.

I walked back toward the mobile phone to place the call, and a few minutes later, while I was discussing the case they'd contacted me about, I felt Russell patting my leg again.

I ignored him until I could hang up.

"Yes, Russell, what is it?"

"I need to call my mother!" he said. "I almost drowned!"

I stared at him. "What do you mean? Did you jump off the diving board again?"

He nodded emphatically.

"Then what happened?"

"I got tired. The lady on the big chair said, 'Are you okay?' and I said, 'No,' so she jumped into the water and saved me."

Oh brother. I looked at Russell, who seemed perfectly fine at this point, and my sons, who were dripping and eager to get back in the water like the little fish they were.

"Okay, well, you can tell her when you get home. But in the meantime, stay in this part of the pool. Boys?"

They all nodded and promised to follow my new rule and I completely forgot to have Russell call home later. The incident slipped my mind until the next morning when I took my boys to the pool again and I felt a familiar pat on my leg.

"Mr. Heird! Mr. Heird! Mr. Heird!"

I looked down to see little blonde Russell with his big brown eyes looking up at me with his usual eager puppy expression.

"Oh hey, Russell. What are you doing here? I thought you couldn't come today?" Dale had invited him but he'd declined. And I knew his mother didn't have a membership at the pool, so I was a bit puzzled.

"We joined the pool! But I can't come with you anymore 'cause last time you almost let me drown."

I looked up to where he was glancing and saw his mother on a lounge chair, glaring at me. Her friend stopped mid conversation and turned to glare at me, too.

Busted.

So I wasn't the perfect multi-tasker. It was like that old Roseanne Barr joke—"If the kids are alive at five, I figure I've done my job." The baby was fine; Jonathan and Billy were happily splashing away—no worries on my part.

I wasn't the type to worry about my boys getting a few scrapes. I wanted them moving and getting exercise and none of them were the type to hide out in their bedrooms and insist they would rather read or do some quiet activity than get outside and do sports. I always had a passion for skiing and wanted to expose my children to skiing, so as my parents had done with me, I started to take Billy, Jonathan, and Andrew on annual family ski vacations.

I also began helicopter skiing on my own once a year starting in 1995. Those helicopter skiing vacations, when I was getting an adrenaline rush and far from the demands of a busy practice and growing family, were incredibly rejuvenating, and a highlight of each year for me. I really needed time away from my "To Do" list, and I didn't know how to make that happen except to go away into the mountains.

It helped that I maintained a high level of physical activity. Here and there, I also fit in some mountain biking—another physical activity that let me work off my frustration, get time to myself, and feel better overall. I ran a triathlon in 1998, and Dale and I took a bike tour through Tuscany, Italy, to celebrate our 15th wedding anniversary in 1999. We attended a Latin mass and jogged through the cobblestone streets near the Leaning Tower of Pisa. I discovered that Dale could jog faster than I could, which irritated me. She decided that she would just leave me in the dust, so to speak.

Later that year, we both participated in the Pittsburgh Marathon, which required a lot of training and provided a distraction for me. Although Dale had bailed on me, I looked forward to the training because it meant spending two or three hours on the weekend running by myself. It was the only time that I had for myself, and it generated a sense of well-being in me. I didn't realize until I was in recovery what a gift it was to have that time devoted just to my pleasure. Now I can appreciate how much I need time when I can simply focus on what I want to do without worrying about whether I might have to run here or there to take care of patients, or tend to someone else's needs.

I didn't stop to reflect much. I was going going going. My daily life had a lot of pressure. Andrew was still a baby in 1995 when I began using prescription painkillers for the first time. It felt like no big deal to me when I tried the samples the pharmaceutical company saleswomen left in my office. I did it once, and then twice—but it happened so rarely that it didn't seem to be a problem. I figured that since I was a physician and very educated about the body and drugs, I was okay. I noticed that if I took the painkillers along with a couple of beers it gave me a nice, warm buzz—a mildly euphoric feeling—and kept me alert. The next day, I would feel fine.

For me, the pills were like a drink—something I could enjoy on the weekends. Then, as the months and even years passed, I started to take them on nights where I wasn't on call. Sometimes, I would go weeks without them, and tell myself I wasn't going back to using them again. But after a stressful day, I would think, *Ah, I'm not on call today, so I don't have to worry about being clear-headed to do surgery. I really need some relief.* For some reason, it wasn't enough to run or bike, or play tennis. I felt I needed, and deserved, to drink a little. So I'd pop a Vicodin and chase it down with some beer.

This went on for several years. Then, by 2000 or so, I was definitely feeling overwhelmed by my professional practice, which was very successful. We were searching for other vascular surgery partners to take some of the pressure off of me and the other vascular surgeon, but there were only about 60 new physicians trained in vascular surgery coming out of training programs each year. I kept thinking, *Once we get another partner, we'll be okay.* But with the shortage of specialists in this field, we couldn't find one.

I felt I was treading water, always overbooked and constantly apologizing to the patients for seeing them a half an hour to 45 minutes or even an hour late. My frustration and helplessness built up. There was no way to scale back, or so it seemed. My patients needed me. My kids needed me. My wife needed me. Heck, even my dog needed me. But I wasn't complaining. I'd chosen this life and all it entailed. I just thought my solution would come in the form of another vascular surgeon joining our practice and until that happened, I'd keep doing my best and hoping something would change. By now, Dale was no longer teaching, but it was still very difficult to juggle everything.

I wished I had more time to coach my boys' teams. I could have been the irritating father in the stand, shouting out criticisms to the coaches, but whatever mistakes they made—or I felt they made—I didn't think it was fair to give them too much grief when I didn't have time to do their jobs. That frustration added to my stress level and, combined with the old "work hard, play hard" mentality, drove me to drink more often. If I was going to go see them play and wasn't on call, I'd drink to relax a little.

Addiction—to the pills, and the alcohol I was chasing them with—was sneaking up on me.

Life went on year after year, with me working harder, always looking ahead to that day when the stress on me was lifted. We'd hire a new vascular surgeon and I'd think, *Oh good—that will take some pressure off.* But the pressure always returned. More and more, I was using pills and alcohol to manage my stress. I felt entitled to do it. It was my little secret. Dale knew I'd have a couple of beers here and there, but she had no idea about the pills.

Then, shortly after 9/11, like so many people, I found myself thinking about what's most important in life. Dale's first cousin had been in the South Tower of the World Trade Center and had gotten out alive. That was sobering. How could we not focus on what was most important when so many people lost their lives suddenly, on the most ordinary of days? An orthopedic surgeon friend had lost his son in Iraq, and at the memorial service, I thought about his son as a cute little blonde boy with curls. Time moved so quickly. It seemed a blanket of sadness wrapped around me. Now, I realize that the alcohol, which is a depressant, was contributing to my dampened mood. At the time, I thought I was just being worn down by the pressures on me. I wanted to think about the future—and have something positive to focus on.

Dale and I got to talking about how much we'd like to have a daughter, and how important it is not to put off what will make you happy. You never know how long your life will be, so waiting until some distant point in the future to do what you want is no way to live—that much we agreed on.

Dale really wanted to adopt a baby girl from China, in part because she wanted to give our love to a girl who would otherwise grow up without a loving home and parents. I shared her feelings to some degree, but I was 44, which made me somewhat hesitant. Did I really want to be a father to a young child again? And there was a part of me that knew I wasn't as happy as I should be in my marriage. Was my life really as stable as it seemed on the surface? At one point, years after recovery, a member of my church said to me that she used to see my family filing into the pews every Sunday, the boys all in polo shirts with their hair neatly combed, our adorable daughter on Dale's hip, and think, *Now that's the perfect family.* She said, "But I guess every family has something going on"—meaning, some secret problem. For us, it was my depression and drug and alcohol use. But I did my best to act the part of the happy, successful suburban dad and keep Dale and the kids in the dark about my prescription drug use.

I decided that Dale's attitude, "life is short," made sense. So while I had my doubts, I let myself be swept along by her determination to adopt a little girl from China. In late 2001 we began the process, which would take quite some time to complete.

In 2003, the SARS epidemic in China prevented us from entering the country, and all adoptions were put on hold. We hadn't chosen a little girl yet, so at least we weren't like some people who had to go through the emotional trauma of not being able to take their daughter home after having met her. Dale and I and the boys prayed at the dinner table every night that we would be united with a little Chinese orphan. Then, in June of 2004, we heard about a toddler who was in good health and up for adoption. Dale got the call while I was at a conference, so I cut the conference short and made the drive to Philadelphia with her. In Philadelphia we talked to the adoption agency director, whose name was Grace. This was the name we had chosen for our little girl.

We knew it was a sign. I smiled at the photo of little Grace. Her head was shaved to prevent lice (infestations were common in Chinese orphanages, we were told) and she was in a walker with her feet propped up as if to say, "Let me out of here already! I have to run!" I instinctively knew she was an active little girl who would fit right in with our family—and my instincts turned out to be right.

Dale and I bought plane tickets to China and got to meet Grace for the first time six weeks later—they wanted us to pick her up in August, which happened to be right when I had two weeks off. Again, it felt as if the universe was shouting to me, "This girl is destined to be your daughter!"

I instantly felt my heart open as soon as I saw Grace, in a room at the orphanage in China. Any doubts about the decision to go forth with Dale's plan were instantly banished. It was love at first sight!

Poor Grace cried with separation anxiety the moment Dale took her in her arms, and my eyes welled up with tears too—only mine were tears of joy. The fact that Grace cried told me she had been cared for with affection, which I was very glad about. The room was bustling with fourteen couples meeting their new daughters, and many of the parents seemed to be crying with pure happiness as the caretakers beamed. A caretaker took bawling Gracie back into her arms and comforted her for a minute or two, and then handed her back to Dale without any protests from our new daughter. And that was the end of Gracie's days at the orphanage.

Grace's passport wouldn't be ready for many days, so we had a wonderful time traveling around China. She quickly adjusted to these two strange people who kept hugging and kissing her, and opened her eyes wide with curiosity as we showed her the sights in the places we traveled to. Some people had advised us to go to Guilin, where we rode in glass bottom boats that took us up the river, where we watched fisherman tying line to cormorants who would then dive for fish, hold them in their mouths, and squawk in protest as the fisherman removed them to be cleaned and eaten later by his family.

We were able to bring Grace home shortly after that, and she blended beautifully into our family. In fact, the older boys were so crazy about their new baby sister that they were eager to feed her and even change her diapers.

All of us were adjusting to the change in our family. But my stress level at work was still very high. My partner and I had attracted one, then two, then three vascular surgeons to help with the workload, and each time I had told myself that being on call less often would make a big difference in my stress. But I continued to feel that life was one big juggling act and if a ball dropped, it would be disastrous for everyone. I couldn't disappoint people, or fail in any way. I was feeling emotionally distant from Dale—our relationship seemed to be about doing things rather than just spending time enjoying each other's company. But I couldn't consider separation or divorce—that was out of the question. To me, divorce would mean I was a failure. No, it was out of the question. I was married for life and I'd have to make the best of it.

And Grace was such a delight. I loved being a father to sons, but there's something special about having a daughter that it's hard to put into words.

And so the years passed, and the insidious disease of addiction crept up on me.

One of the side effects of using alcohol is it can cause depression. It lifts you up as soon as it hits your dopamine receptors, but then, because you're artificially stimulating the pleasure centers in your brain, there's a drop off afterward. You feel down again, and crave the alcohol because you know it will make you feel good again. I was chasing after that euphoric feeling of my college fraternity days: the feeling of sitting in the late afternoon sunshine, flirting with pretty girls in sundresses, with KC and the Sunshine Band singing. Alcohol was my sun. The painkillers were simply the catalyst that allowed me to enjoy my beer, or gin and tonic, or wine, without having to pay the price of the hangover or sleepiness.

Toward the mid-2000s, I started to experience withdrawal symptoms. I knew I had developed a dependence. I even went cold turkey for a while in the summer of 2005, pushing through the discomfort of fatigue, achiness, runny nose, and jitteriness. That withdrawal, the summer of 2005, should have woken me up. But one Sunday afternoon a couple of weeks later, it seemed like a good idea to take a pill to keep myself chugging along. Even as I was swallowing two pills, there was a voice inside me that said, "Nooooo!" but it didn't stop me. I knew I would quickly become dependent again and not be able to stop without help.

So what was I thinking? My executive function, the part of the brain that controls impulses and engages in long-term planning, was just not online. I just wanted the pills, *now!* I didn't want to think past that point.

Later, I wrote that first prescription for Percocets in Dale's name, and then switched to Vicodin pills so that the pharmacists wouldn't catch on to the number of prescriptions I was writing. I knew what I was doing was wrong, but I justified it to myself.

This was the pattern that continued until the addiction became so strong that I couldn't stop. The physical withdrawal symptoms became so severe that I was not really taking the drug to get relief from anything but those symptoms. By then, I was totally powerless. I needed help then, but didn't have the courage to ask for it. I felt increasingly isolated, and scared that someone would find out what I was doing.

But I couldn't escape the dark feeling of hopelessness that my drinking was creating in me. At best, I could dull the frustration and depression by distracting myself, but the feelings would come back. I distinctly remember driving to one of my son's baseball games a sunny spring day just a few weeks before the DEA came after me. I opened the door to my car to get out, and smelled the freshly mown grass, and thought, *I use to love that smell.* I inhaled its fragrance, but the feelings of joy and comfort it used to evoke in me weren't there. I sat for a moment, motionless, and felt myself choke up. What had happened to the kid who ran around his parents' farm, delighting in the smells and the sounds of spring each year, feeling the grass between his toes as he ran across the fields to the pond? I felt completely isolated—from everyone. And from God. The source of my joy seemed to have dried up, and a part of me had died. My sense of sadness and emptiness threatened to engulf me. In the distance, I heard the sound of a bat cracking against a ball and the crowd cheering in the field. "Oh God," I began to pray. "I don't know what's happened, but if just once more, just once more, I could just feel that feeling I used to have when I smelled freshly cut grass…" If. What was I missing? I was doing everything right but feeling so lost and alone.

I'll feel better when I see Andrew in his uniform, playing, I thought. I tried to shake off the dark feeling, but I couldn't. I spent the entire game in the car, stuck. My life was stuck. I couldn't think about Andrew.

Being around my kids always lifted me up. In fact, it was the only thing I was able to enjoy. But it was as if I'd lost the capacity to feel happiness. Later that week, a tennis match of Billy's got postponed by rain, and I had to be on call for a patient who was likely to need emergency surgery any minute. I had just finished another surgery, but when Billy called to let me know that they had rescheduled the match for 8:00 p.m. now that the rain had stopped, I had to tell him I couldn't come. The match was an hour away, which was too far if this patient needed me pronto.

If I had been in touch with my feelings, I would say I resented being in that situation. I wanted to be there to support Billy. I wanted to be a good dad. And I wanted to do the one thing that day that would give me joy. But I couldn't. So I drank a beer—just one.

Then the call came. *Damn!* I had to do the surgery after all.

I was very focused—it was a surgery I had done many, many times—and I did perfect work. But the nurse who was assisting smelled alcohol on my breath and unknown to me, reported it to the director of the hospital.

He called me in the next day, and I admitted that I'd had one beer—and explained the circumstances.

"Do you have a drinking problem?" he asked.

No, I have a drug problem. I didn't say that, though I thought it.

"No. It really was just a bad choice this one time. I was just so frustrated about missing my son's game." I thought, *Don't German doctors drink a beer between cases?* I felt it was no big deal. But all I said was, "I won't do it again. You have my word."

I thought I could simply stop, but I was getting flu-like symptoms when the drug wasn't in my body: I had aches, a runny nose, and a jittery feeling. Of course, as a doctor, I knew those were withdrawal symptoms, which meant I'd developed a dependency on the drugs. My mind said, "I really should stop taking these," but then I would always find a reason to take them again.

Eleven years of crescendoing drug and alcohol use had created a monster I couldn't tame. I had reached a breaking point.

Chapter Eighteen # Detox

ervousness, fear, and embarrassment were all mixed together in me that day when the DEA agents showed up. But the most powerful emotions I felt were relief and hope. I knew I had a problem. Acknowledging it was like taking off a heavy coat that was weighing me down. And I was tired of the deception. At last, I was going to get help and stop feeling trapped by my addiction—a dependency that was undeniable for a physician like me, who had read all the side effects of the medications and knew all the signs of chemical dependency. I didn't know much about what rehab involved, but I knew it was right for me.

That's not to say that I was skipping into the rehab facility. I was *not* looking forward to Phase One on the detox floor, which I knew would entail 72 hours of careful medical observation—and me feeling physically miserable. The medical observation was important as there would be a risk of delirium tremens, stroke, heart attack, or seizure as my body adjusted to being without alcohol—or painkillers—in my system. By this point,

I was drinking three to six beers, combining them with a dozen or so Vicodin, over the course of a day. The alcohol withdrawal alone might set off delirium tremens, which can lead to seizures and even death if not supervised by a physician and treated with medical protocols. I believed I would be safe, but I knew I'd feel awful.

Following the departure of the drug enforcement agents, Dale and I finished packing up our car and drove the two-and-a-half hours to Waverly, Pennsylvania, where Marworth Treatment Center was located. I had called them earlier in the day and they checked my insurance coverage, and then confirmed that I would be admitted. I knew that my policy would probably not cover my full stay if I followed Dr. Stefan's advice and remained in rehab as long as I needed to, but I could deal with the financial repercussions of that later. My life was on the line. I was determined to do what it took to become sober.

I had hit rock bottom, as they say in recovery programs, so I didn't need any coaxing or cajoling to face my addictions. The same drive that had propelled me to become an A student, get into medical school, and complete my surgeon's training and certification—the drive that made me get up and go for a run when I could easily have just given in to the desire to take a nap—was making me eager to get started with the process of recovery. At the same time, my emotions were all over the place as my mind raced. How would my kids and my parents react once the news hit the papers—and the Internet? What would happen with my practice? How would my clients feel when they found out?

I knew I'd be attending some sort of meetings while I was in rehab, and I would have to talk about the decisions I'd made and why I'd made them. Beyond that, I'd have to see what was involved. What goes on in rehab was a mystery to me.

On the trip up to Waverly, I made phone calls to my office and told them I would need an unspecified amount of time to get treatment for painkiller addiction. At this point, I honestly had no idea I was addicted to alcohol, too. The way I saw it, I was only drinking beer to enhance the painkiller high. I didn't see it as a problem on its own, and didn't think to tell them anything about my drinking.

I knew I would have to be gone for up to 90 days, so my plan was to pick a date in mid-September to return to the office. One of my partners was overseas, so I didn't talk to him directly, but I did speak to the office assistants and my other partner. Everyone seemed supportive, which was helpful given my emotional state. I was trying to hold it together, but the whirl of feelings was like a storm brewing within me. I looked out the window at the greenery along the road. Everything was in bloom—the trees, the flowers. A new start. That's what I needed. I had to focus on my recovery right now. For the next three days, I wouldn't even be able to talk to my wife, much less deal with medical emergencies that any of my patients experienced. I would be on the detox floor, unable to take or make calls.

When I'd contacted my father and mother the night before, I told them I was sick and was going to have to go to a rehab center because I'd become addicted to painkillers. I started to explain that I was potentially facing legal problems, too, but that seemed to confuse them, so I chose not to expose them to any more details. I didn't want to create any more anxiety for them, so I just reassured them that I had an excellent lawyer and that they shouldn't worry.

Then, I called my brother and told him the situation. "I'm going to be in rehab the day of Billy's high school graduation," I said. "Could you stand in for me?"

"Absolutely," he said. "You do what you need to do. You can count on me."

That's my family. Just as when I'd been in that serious car accident, they were completely supportive, and ready to take whatever action needed to help me out. I know not everyone with an addiction is as fortunate as I am to have that level of support. I will always be grateful for my incredible family.

I also called the Physicians' Health Program of Pennsylvania, which several people had told me to do. It's a program for physicians to help them in the face of addiction. They monitor and keep track of your urine to ensure you're not slipping up and using drugs or alcohol again. They also require you to check in with them regularly, and help you to find the resources you need to get well and stay well. And they will confirm for the medical board or your insurance companies that you are maintaining sobriety. The experience of trying to deal with my addiction by myself unsuccessfully gave me a hint about how important it was to get support in recovery. The addictive thinking makes you want to believe you can do it alone, but you really do need help.

Marworth Treatment Center is a mansion on top of a hill in the rolling hills north of Scranton, Pennsylvania, surrounded by trees, with a southern view of the Pennsylvania hillside. The mansion had been donated by a woman, Mary Worthington, who wanted it to be converted into a rehabilitation center. As we pulled into the front parking lot, I was glad it was a natural setting. Being outside, seeing the sky and trees, hearing the robins and cardinals calling to each other instead of being stuck in hospital and meeting rooms at all times, would make me feel better. We walked into a well-kept waiting area with lots of big Queen Anne leather chairs and a large library.

I then carried through with a classic addict's ritual—although I didn't know how clichéd my behavior was—I got myself to a private area, the guest bathroom, to take my drugs one last time. A few Vicodins would delay any withdrawal symptoms for at least another four hours, which meant four more hours without the aches, the runny nose, and the jittery feeling I hated. At this point, taking drugs and alcohol didn't make me high anymore. It just allowed me to function without feeling awful physically. I'd been instructed to bring all of my pills along, which included Vicodin, Soma Compound with Codeine, Tylenol #3, and Valium. I used the Valium to help me sleep and the Soma Compound and Tylenol to keep the Vicodin withdrawal symptoms under control. I'd be asked to turn in my bag of medications.

It's interesting to me that my first day of sobriety—May 25, 2006—mirrored the date I graduated from medical school training. Synchronicities like this meant nothing to me at the time, but now I ponder their meaning. Do they exist because we're supposed to slow down, think about these coincidences, and make connections between the events of our lives, observing patterns? Now, I would notice the date. That day, my thoughts were on getting through detox.

I kissed Dale good-bye and told her I'd check in with her when I came out of the three-day blackout period of detox and was allowed to make phone calls again—although they would have to be short, I was instructed. That would be Memorial Day weekend, and I knew she had plans with the kids. Next, I was escorted back to the intake area with a nurse who drew blood. I gave her a urine sample, and she began to take my vital signs as part of a physical exam before I headed to the detox floor.

I learned I would share a room with another newcomer. Once the nurse left me there, I didn't have much to do but think ... and feel. Reality was setting in. The thoughts swirled in my head. *What happened to me? What have I done? What about my family, my parents, the practice, my livelihood, my business, everything that I had worked so hard for, for so many years?* I knew my identity as a successful surgeon, father, husband—you name it—was in jeopardy. *What will people think of me?*

I started crying as the sadness, shame, fear, blame, and remorse surfaced. Then, the withdrawal symptoms arrived: restlessness, achiness, severe abdominal cramps, diarrhea, and, that night, insomnia.

On the second day, I was allowed to have Suboxone, a medication that blocks the morphine receptors and binds to them. It doesn't make you high, but it gives you relief from the withdrawal symptoms, which was just what I needed. Then, things settled down for me physically. The Sunday morning of Memorial Day weekend, I woke up for the first time in many, many months feeling normal—not high, not numb, not cloudy, just normal. It was a beautiful, warm, sunny morning, and I was allowed to walk out onto a large patio behind the dining area. I sat there, basking, just observing the lawn and listening to the sounds of nature. A trio of deer appeared at the edge of the wood and quietly trotted across the lawn and out of my sight.

Wow, do I feel good! I smiled. It was great to feel physically normal again.

But soon after that, my darker feelings came back to me. I could feel my blood pressure rising. *What the hell happened? How did I get here? I'm sitting in a rehab hospital, which is really just the same as a psychiatric hospital—for crazy people.* I felt as if I'd stepped into the movie *One Flew Over the Cuckoo's Nest.* This experience was *not* in my plan for my life!

When had I last sat down quietly and simply reflected on my life? I couldn't remember. No wonder so many emotions and thoughts were coming up! But the remorse and irritation with myself started to be replaced with feelings of hope. After many years of never looking at myself and taking care of myself, I was finally going to have an opportunity to take care of Steve. I almost laughed with relief. *Steve, the perfect physician, father, husband—Steve gets to come first for once?* All the other things— family and business and patients—were going to have to wait. It seems obvious now that I had put my needs last, behind everyone else's, to the point where I'd pretty much forgotten what they were, for years, and deadened myself.

Alcohol and drug addiction starts out as habits you can control, but soon, these substances are in control of you. For a long time, the pills and alcohol I depended on made me feel present in the moment. They let me feel good in my body, and gave me a sense of calmness and alertness that I really enjoyed. Then, they simply kept me going. And the whole time, they were robbing me of my sense of connection—to other people, to nature, to God. I began to feel increasingly isolated and disconnected. It was almost as if the flow of my life force was being slowly constricted. I was the expert at clearing arteries and veins, making repairs, doing bypasses. I could get my patient's blood flowing freely again. But I had lost my ability to let my own life force, that incredible gift from God, flow freely. Physician, heal thyself!

Through my tears, I saw the face of a fellow patient who had taken a seat near me. He had a ruddy complexion and blonde hair and looked at me with a gentle smile, as if to say, "Been there. I know."

Ugh. Given how miserable I was, his smile annoyed me.

I wiped my tears with the back of my hand.

The fellow didn't leave. He seemed to have appeared from nowhere, and was the only other person around. *Maybe I ought to at least say hello…*

"Hey. I'm Steve," I said finally, remembering my manners and holding up my hand in greeting.

"I'm Jack. Just arrived?"

I nodded. Then, my feelings just poured out of me. "I've never felt this horrible. I never want to feel this way again."

He sat quietly.

"What do I have to do to never feel this way again?"

His eyes looked into mine without judgment. "Change."

"Change what?"

"Everything," he said.

Everything. Yeah, no problem.

I took a deep breath. *If that's what it will take, then, okay.* It was a moment of pure surrender. What other choice did I have? Misery can be an incredible motivator.

The detox was beginning. What I didn't realize was I had a lot of poisonous beliefs and behavior patterns that I was going to have to detox from as well.

Chapter Nineteen   Heal Thyself

T he physicians treating me were tapering my doses of Suboxone based upon their routine narcotic withdrawal protocol, and after three days, my symptoms subsided.

I was able to sit out on the lawn, or in the big, glass-enclosed meeting room where I could look out at the grass, trees, and sky, but much of my time was spent on the detox floor where I was getting medical treatment. The floor was more hospital-like than residential and seemed the appropriate place for a man who looked like he had just come from skid row: haggard, disheveled, and bearded, with dirty skin that seemed to have been exposed to the elements for years and clothes so filthy he smelled. He told me his name was John and he was a professor, but he was so dirty, and seemed mentally out of it, that I thought, *Wow, I wonder if he has what they call "wet brain?"* Wet brain is a serious complication of long-term alcoholism that involves irreversible brain damage. I didn't see John much for the next few weeks.

I was told I would be in detox about seven days. I'd be in over the Memorial Day weekend and move to a residential floor a few days after that. I began getting used to the ward, but it was still odd to me to be there and be stripped of my identity, or what I considered my identity. For instance, as a physician, I was used to being able to step around the nurses' side of the counter, and now I was on the other side of it. It's a little thing, but a constant reminder that I had become the patient, just another person with an addiction. It was disorienting.

Already, I was starting to learn about the disease of addiction, which has physical, mental, emotional, and spiritual aspects. I found out that even though I'd thought it was only painkillers I was addicted to, I wouldn't be able to drink anymore. That surprised me. I didn't have cravings for alcohol, for one thing. I didn't develop any delirium tremens thanks to the high quality medical care. I'm not sure I was in great danger of it, because I hadn't done binge drinking in years, but there are no guarantees that even a medically monitored detox will prevent dangerous withdrawal symptoms.

I learned that I was what they call cross addicted. Using one drug would tempt me to use the other, and all drugs, including alcohol, can lead to dependence or addiction. Distorted thinking, or stinking thinking, as they say, drives you to justify the misuse of these substances. Of course, I didn't want to believe all that. I wanted to believe I could control my alcohol use and be a casual, social drinker when I got out, but the doctors made it clear they knew better and I was kidding myself. Although I was a physician, my training in the effects of drugs and alcohol was minimal. I had to admit that I was not the expert here.

And besides, ever since that day when I was crying and Jack, the other patient, quietly spoke the truth about what I was going to have to do, I had realized I was willing to change everything. Had my life become unmanageable? Absolutely. If drinking was going to have to be a thing of the past, I could accept that.

After three days in detox, I decided to stop taking the Suboxone. I was feeling so well that I thought I could do without it. My attitude was that I came to rehab to get off of pills, so don't give me any pills!

It was that old ambition driving me. The doctors disagreed with my decision—"I think you'll regret it," I was told. But because it was medically safe for me to stop the medication at that point, they respected my wishes. Maybe they knew more than I did about what AA calls Good Orderly Direction, or G.O.D.—that is another way of thinking about the Higher Power you have to surrender to. God, or G.O.D., has ways of waking us up to what we need to discover, and what I needed to discover was that I had to get my ego out of the way and follow the doctors' orders. Within 24 hours, I started to get a runny nose and experiencing aches and pains. These were classic symptoms of withdrawal from painkillers, but I was in my ego and convinced that I was just developing a cold. "Ah, this won't be so bad," I told myself as I went to sleep that night.

By 2:00 a.m., I was experiencing severe cramps, insomnia, and restlessness. I was congested and sneezing, and my nose was running. I had been reading some of the AA literature while I was in detox, and I had just learned my first lesson: When you don't surrender, you suffer. I'd decided to let my will guide my decisions instead of letting Good, Orderly Direction guide me. And now, the withdrawal symptoms were kicking my butt. *Okay, I need to totally let go here and listen to the doctors, and let others guide me, until I'm well enough to start making sound decisions for myself again.*

I got out of bed and went to find the night nurse. I begged him for a Suboxone pill, explaining my situation and the insight I'd just had. With reluctance—because there was no doctor around to give approval—he gave me a Suboxone.

In about ten minutes, I felt relief from the withdrawal symptoms. I fell back to sleep and woke up the next day with a more enlightened attitude about following instructions, advice, and directions from everyone around me.

It's a good thing I'd edged my ego out of the way—as they say, EGO means "edging God out," and that's what I was doing when I let my will run the show instead of submitting to the will of my Higher Power. I had given in to my ego and had a miserable night.

After seven days on the detox floor, I was ready for my next stage of recovery. First, however, I wanted to check in at home. I called Dale to let her know the news and find out how it had gone with my son, Billy. I had not only missed his graduation but his all-important tennis state tennis match. He'd won! I told her to tell him that I was very proud of him. Then, I explained I was going to start group therapy and twelve-step meetings to deal with my addiction. I told her that I'd begun reading some of the literature and realized I had to change a lot—basically, everything, from my thinking to my behavior patterns … It was a lot but I was feeling good again. Hopeful. And ready to do the hard work ahead of me.

"So," she said, trying to take in all that I was saying in my state of eagerness, "are you going to be able to drink again when you get home?"

"No. Not even one beer. Those days are behind me. See, it's all connected—the drugs, the alcohol, the addiction to not dealing with my feelings. I'm learning a lot. But yeah, they made it absolutely clear. No alcohol."

I knew that would be an adjustment for her. She liked her wine over dinner, or while chatting with friends. If I couldn't be a part of having a little beer or wine, that was going to be a big change. We didn't have time to talk about what our social life or weekends would look like with me not imbibing. I imagine she did some thinking about that while I was in rehab.

Dale wanted to support me. That was clear. We were a family, she was committed to being married, which meant that whatever it took to heal our family, she would do her best to get it done. But like many spouses of addicts, she had no idea what she was in for, or how much I would change—and how much our relationship would change as a consequence.

Truthfully, our relationship had been in trouble for years—maybe not from her perspective, but from mine. I just wasn't happy. I could see she wasn't happy. But in my mind, marriage is forever. You make that commitment in front of God, your family, and friends, and you stick to it, for better or worse. If my marriage were to fail, then that meant I was a failure, a failure at sticking to my commitment and vows. In a way, that was good, because it meant I gave my marriage all that I could. It also meant that despite my doubts about whether Dale and I could be happy together—and despite my doubts about bringing another child into our home given the state of our marriage—I had gone along with Dale's plan to adopt a girl from China. I wouldn't have had my incredible daughter, Grace, if I hadn't been so committed to my marriage and our family. And frankly, I might not have had her if I'd been sober, because after I went through rehab, one of my most profound changes was being more assertive about my own needs and feelings. If we'd had the discussion about adopting at that point in my life, instead of years before, I would have strongly indicated my feelings of doubt to Dale about her plan to adopt. So despite the pain addiction caused me and my family, despite the losses it led to, it gave me the precious gift of my daughter. And I wouldn't trade that for anything. Now, when things seem bad, I try to remember that wonderful things can come out of the worst situations.

But back to rehab. The daily life in a rehab facility is very structured, with lots of rules, some of which may seem, on the surface, to be nitpicky. One of the reasons for that is addiction and alcoholism take people into self-destructive behaviors. Addiction leads to death. It may take years before you destroy your body, or end up in a fatal car crash caused by drunk driving, but you die of the disease earlier than you would have if you had gotten treatment. Addicts make poor choices and have trouble following instructions. They need to relearn to follow the rules instead of constantly crossing society's boundaries and thinking the rules didn't apply to them. I could understand that intellectually, but before I left rehab, I would have to learn it through experience, too.

It was challenging to meet all the rules and regulations, but I'm good at figuring out how to juggle responsibilities and make situations work, so I knew I would be okay. When my detox was done, I was assigned a counselor who did a thorough interview with me. I was also administered a personality test and interviewed by a psychologist as well as an addictionologist, an MD who specializes in addiction therapy.

And before I left the detox floor, that first Sunday evening, I began some of the therapy sessions. I remember that on Monday, which was Memorial Day, I had an art therapy session where we drew and painted. I hadn't done anything like that since I was a kid. It was a little awkward at first, but then I could see the point of it. They were teaching us to get in touch with our creativity, expressing ourselves in healthy ways, once again instead of drinking or drugging to repress feelings. I had to learn how to enjoy simple pleasures again.

The rehab center emphasized working with a twelve-step program and I started by working on the first three steps:

1. We admitted we were powerless over our addiction—that our lives had become unmanageable.
2. Came to believe a Power greater than ourselves could restore us to sanity.
3. Made a decision to turn our will and our lives over to the care of God, as we understood him.

I was excited to know that this was a spiritual recovery program. In my younger years, I had always believed in God. I was raised Methodist and had been involved in Sunday school since I was a toddler, participating in the junior choir at church from the age of six through junior high school. I had been married in the Catholic church—I didn't convert, but I did agree that our children would be raised Catholic, so all of us went to mass every Sunday. I had no trouble identifying my "Higher Power" as God. And I was comfortable turning over my will to Him, although of course, as with most things, there's your intention, which is easy to set, and then there's actually following through on your intention, which is an entirely different challenge. It is really difficult for an addict to give up the addiction to the belief "I can handle this—I can trust my own decision making." Eh, not so much! Many addicts have to experience again and again the humbling reality that whenever you embrace that stinking thinking instead of submitting to the guidance and will of your Higher Power, you do something stupid or make a bad decision.

Fortunately, because I already had a relationship with God, whenever the one-ton weight dropped on my head and I realized oops, I let my ego get the better of me and edged God out again, I was able to self-correct and trust in my Higher Power to guide me. In rehab it felt good to renew my relationship with God—to pray again and feel that God was listening. I hadn't realized how much I missed that.

Rehab also featured behavioral modification programs for assisting us in changing our thinking, modifying our reactions, and taking charge of our emotions. Like many people in rehab with me, I had long forgotten what it was like to experience my emotions and express them. That was something I was going to have to relearn.

There was also small-group therapy, which I did with other physicians who were in for drug and/or alcohol addiction, and there were evening programs, such as twelve-step meetings and lectures. Those programs were segregated by gender. It's common for people in addiction to avoid doing the work of recovery by getting romantically or sexually involved with others, so there was a lot of gender separation to prevent that distraction.

Within the rehab program, there was a subgroup of patients that were part of the Port Authority of New York City. The Port Authority of New York City had a contract with Marworth, so the rehab had many police officers, firefighters, and transit workers who needed to overcome an addiction. From what these patients said, the stresses of those jobs were a big factor in their developing the habit of drinking or drugging for stress relief. I could definitely relate to that. Being on call all of the time, feeling that I always had to be on alert for an emergency where someone's life could hang in the balance, was creating stress for me that was like a low-grade fever. There was no escaping it considering the nature of my work.

I was beginning to learn that by listening to others' stories, I could discover common experiences, which made me feel less isolated. The isolation of addiction is dangerous. We pull away from people who care about us, and from God (although, of course, a lot of people don't have a relationship with God to begin with, which can make recovery even harder for them).

My first roommate was a lieutenant in the New York City Police Department. He was discharged after three days—I'm not sure why—and was replaced by a young medical student who was in rehab to deal with his alcoholism. This medical student became my roommate for the next two weeks. As uncomfortable as it was to have to share what was, essentially, a dorm room, with a stranger, they all seemed to be nice guys. I felt somewhat of a connection to the med student because I knew what the pressures of medical training are like.

My new roommate told me that his loved ones had performed an intervention to get him into rehab, which he didn't seem happy about. I came to learn that when this is the situation, the addicted person is more likely to relapse than if he came to rehab entirely on his own steam. Even so, I think it's important to try to get your loved one into rehab anyway— not only for that person but also for yourself. If something terrible were to happen—a car accident, cardiac arrest caused by chronic drinking, or some other alcohol related disaster—at least you would know that you did what you could to stop the destructive behavior. There are no guarantees with rehab, but without it, an alcoholic or drug addict is guaranteed to have a lower quality of life and die earlier because of the addiction.

As I settled into the routine of Marworth, my feelings of relief and hopefulness grew stronger. The pressures of my everyday life were gone, and I could focus on getting well. It was easier to pay attention to what I was experiencing, although I was clearly rusty at identifying my feelings. I had squelched them so much over the years in order to protect other peoples' feelings, or not inconvenience them, that I had a lot of work ahead of me when it came to reawakening to my emotions.

The following weekend, when Dale came to visit, I had a moment where I realized that despite my commitment to getting better, I really did have a compulsion to use drugs again. I said hello to her, she gave me a peck on the lips. Almost immediately, she handed me a small packet of documents from home for me to sign and began talking about all of the problems she was dealing with, in my absence. We sat down at one of the four wooden, square tables in the dining hall area, basking in the sunlight that was streaming through several windows that faced the grounds' gardens. As Dale went through her list of challenges, I felt a strong urge to reach my hand up to my mouth and throw pills into it to get a sense of relief. In fact, I performed the motion in my mind—it was that strong an impulse.

This was the first time I felt the urge to take a drug and it scared me. Clearly, my drug use wasn't just about feeling a buzz, as I'd told myself before I stopped feeling that mild euphoria about eighteen months prior to rehab. It was about something deeper, something to do with my sense of feeling that my life had spun out of my control. The pressures were like a precarious pile about to topple over and bury me.

In that moment, I recognized that my wife was a trigger for me. In other words, being with her put me at risk of relapse. Being around her made me feel anxious—and anxiety, I'd learned, was a big risk for relapse. I had a lot of work to do to develop my ability to cope with stress before I was ready to come home, that was certain.

As we talked, Dale made it clear that the boys were rallying to hold our family together for the next few months. "We'll hang in there for you, Steve," she told me. I sensed that she felt that once I got this "rehab thing" out of the way, everything would be perfect. Everything would go back to the way it was when I left only I wouldn't be using drugs—or alcohol.

But already, I knew that wasn't true. I couldn't say how things would change. I only knew that what I was experiencing was so powerful, so different from what I'd been going through for years and years, that my life was going to transform—for the better. What exactly that would look like and how the changes would affect my family, I didn't know. But I believed that whatever the change was, it would be good.

As I did the work of recovery, my sense of hopefulness increased. I could feel that I was getting back in touch with who I really was, underneath all the activities that seemed to define me. I felt reconnected with God. It could only get better from here!

And I didn't miss the pills, or even the alcohol. Giving up beer after work seemed doable. I was learning new ways to deal with stress. I realized I had already discovered some excellent techniques for self-nurturing over the years. I just hadn't valued myself and my emotions enough to use them regularly. For instance, I loved to run and to helicopter ski. By allowing myself to do those things without allowing them to become soft addictions—distractions from my feelings—I could manage my stress.

Physical activities I loved would help me avoid drugs and alcohol one day at a time, as they say.

I still had a ways to go to overcome my addiction to pleasing other people, though. Trying to make people like me and be happy was what's called a "soft addiction" for me. My compulsion to be the guy that everyone likes and that makes everyone happy distracted me from my own uncomfortable feelings like resentment, sadness, frustration, worry, and anger. Those emotions exist for a reason, the same way that pain does. If you're in pain, it's a signal that there's something wrong. A good medical intake interview involves asking the patient about pain. When did it start? What type of pain is it? How would you rate it on a scale of 1 to 10? We don't ask patients about emotional pain, or mental or spiritual distress. It didn't occur to me that I was in an emotional, mental, and spiritual crisis because I had no idea what the signs were. All I knew was that I was physically addicted to painkillers, and for some bizarre reason I couldn't explain, I went back to them even after I broke through the physical withdrawal a few months before rehab. I had actually suffered through the withdrawal, telling my wife I must have a cold or flu or something, and gotten off the pills. Yet I went back, which baffled me. Now I realized I was self-medicating for pain that wasn't physical.

An example of how much of a people pleaser I was? When I first came to rehab, I knew my son Billy was set to graduate June 9. To my surprise, I was told by my rehab counselors that I would be granted a one-time, one-day pass to attend. I started to think about it, though. Was it a good idea? I trusted myself not to drink or use painkillers—not that I had any, because I'd handed them in when I entered rehab, but people with addictions find ways to obtain these things if they're desperate for them. My brother had already committed to attending in my place, Dale had a specific number of tickets for the ceremony and a reservation at the restaurant. All the plans were set. No, I decided, it would probably be best if I just remained in rehab that day and let everyone in the family stick with the plan.

Now that I'm further along in recovery, I can see what I was doing when going through this mental process: I was trying, as always, to keep everyone happy even if it meant denying my own emotional needs. I didn't want to make Dale irritated or anxious. I didn't want to upset anyone. Maybe the "he's coming, he's not coming, no, he's coming" emotional roller coaster *would* ruin things for Billy. But today, I would take the time to consider where my decision was coming from: the actual emotional needs of everyone involved, including myself, or the old habit of not making any waves so as to avoid conflict. I'd be able to more clearly see that Billy would rather have me there if I could make it. But I was still in the early stages of recovery at this point, and my addictive thinking—*I can't upset anyone! I can't risk anyone being mad at me!*—prevailed.

About three weeks into the program, I was scheduled to attend a meeting to get me ready for the next stage of rehab after the traditional inpatient program. Phase Two was implemented when the committee of counselors and addictionologists decided that you were well enough and trustworthy enough to go to outside twelve-step meetings. In Phase Two, you'd call and request rides from other members of these support groups rather than going in a van with the other patients at Marworth. Not only did this give us more independence to ready us for discharge but also test us on our ability to follow the rules, to trust in others who were committed to working the twelve steps. My 50th birthday was coming up on July 2, and I was hoping to return home by then for a short visit to celebrate my birthday and be back with my family.

Some of the men who had been in the program for 28 days because their insurance covered their inpatient treatment for exactly that long were being discharged the following day. I knew some of them probably should have stayed longer, but they didn't have the money to remain in rehab. At least they had 28 days' coverage, which was better than nothing I guess. Some of the patients only had a week or so covered, and I suspected they would end up back in rehab at some point. You can't really make much progress in such a short time frame. The soon-to-be-released patients would be getting up to explain their experience of working the second step of our twelve-step program: Came to believe that a power greater than yourself could restore you to sanity. The idea was that each person who was speaking would explain in his own words how he saw his Higher Power working in his life today.

I watched as one of the men walked up to the podium: It was John, the alcoholic professor I had seen in the detox unit a couple of weeks before. I was shocked to see him looking so good. John was spic and span, nothing like how he was on the detox floor: freshly shaved, his hair clean and neat, his clothes no longer rumpled. He had a spring in his step as he walked up to the podium. Soon after he started his story, he mentioned he was going to be discharged the next day. Now, I'd run into him a couple of times in rehab, for just a few brief moments, but with fifty or sixty people in rehab, and him in another group, I really hadn't seen him enough to notice whether he still showed signs of possibly having wet brain. As he spoke, I saw that clearly, he had escaped that horrible complication of alcoholism. As he stood up there, a glow came from within him. He talked about how he saw God working in his life, and about the relationship he had with his Higher Power.

I stared at him in disbelief. I couldn't get over his profound transformation. I almost didn't recognize him because he looked so different.

When John finished speaking, we were asked if we had any comments. I rose and said, "John, I remember when you came into the detox unit. I see what you look like and sound like now, and I don't know what has happened to you, but I want what you have." I sat down, and he acknowledged what I said with a smile and a nod.

I have come to believe that you receive what you request and what you pray for. Within six hours of that declaration, I experienced the most profound and mysterious event in my life. In a way, it's as if my life were divided into two halves, the time before that night and the time after my awakening.

Chapter Twenty

The Awakening

After the meeting, I went to bed as usual in my shared rehab room. But then, I woke up in the middle of the night with the recognition that I was still experiencing some withdrawal symptoms. For one thing, I was especially sensitive to the fact that the room was cold. The air conditioning had been turned on at the request of the patients, who were feeling uncomfortably warm during a several-day-long heat wave in Northern Pennsylvania. The janitor warned us that we'd regret the choice to switch the heat to air conditioning once the cool weather typical of the area this time of year returned, but like fools, we didn't listen to him. Now, I shivered as I quietly turned on the bedside reading lamp so as not to disturb my roommate. He was sleeping soundly as he seemed to every night, while I was clearly experiencing insomnia—a withdrawal symptom. I knew I'd be tossing and turning for an hour or two if I tried to go back to sleep, so I decided to do some reading.

I had a very small stack of books on my nightstand and selected a blue-and-white paperback that was only about twenty-three pages long, which I had read several times already. As I recall, the title was something like *Acceptance and Surrender*—a reference to the fact that to recover from addiction, you have to surrender to a Higher Power and accept things just as they are without resentment or regret. I settled back into bed, opened the book, and turned my body and the book toward the light.

I read about how there is always something to find to be grateful for, so when something bad or annoying happens, you should look at the positive side of it—for example, if the meow of a cat awakes you in the middle of the night, be grateful for having healthy hearing so you can hear a cat's meow, because not everyone can hear. I thought about this idea of always finding a reason to be grateful for every experience. Was I grateful to be safe from my secret and lonely world of addiction? Yes, I was grateful. I was grateful to be getting help.

This small thought of gratitude seemed to create the smallest crack of light in my consciousness. My mind's eye began to experience a stream of images. Pictures of my past experiences created a montage of memories. Some of the pictures were of past events I was holding myself accountable for, and in the past, they made me feel guilty, ashamed, and culpable— as if they were evidence that I had failed somehow. But I was now the observer of these events, and had clarity about what I'd experienced. I realized that while the outcomes were not necessarily what I'd intended or desired, I had done the best I could and many of the outcomes were beyond my control.

This realization opened the floodgates of memories. Time seemed to stand still as memory after memory flowed past, each causing me to have the same realization that I had done the best I could at the time given what I knew and where I was in my emotional and spiritual development. I felt I could let go of the burdens of guilt and shame over the outcomes. Many of these events were poor surgical outcomes, but others were life experiences such as disappointing my family because I was working too much and abusing painkillers and alcohol. All the numbness I had felt for years, the protective shell that hid my painful emotions, was slowly melting away like an ice cube exposed to the warmth of bright sunlight.

There were other memories flowing past in the opposite direction, memories of responsibilities I had ignored or minimized that in reality were significant. I knew I needed to take responsibility for neglecting them. It was now time for me to face the truth that I had been avoiding—and the truth that despite all I'd done that made me feel bad about myself, despite the mistakes I'd made, I was lovable, and I was loved for just being me. This love was coming to me from God, who was granting me grace. I understood at last what grace really means—undeserved but overwhelming love, forgiveness, and acceptance.

As the pictures of past events continued to flow in both directions, with me as the observer, I felt released from any emotional attachments to the past. A sense of freedom and love slowly descended upon me and grew in intensity until I felt myself crying tears of joy. The warm, embracing feeling of love that was surrounding me was filling me up, filling spaces in me that had been dark and empty.

I crawled out of bed and quietly walked across the dark room into the small bathroom. The presence of unconditional love continued to grow around me and in me, welling up out of the center of my chest. Somehow, I knew "I am worthy of love just the way I am," that love isn't something I needed to earn but is always available to me. All I needed to do was to open my heart to this truth and the love would flow.

I was overcome with joy. My tears flowed. *I'm okay just the way I am? I don't need to do anything to be loved? I'm loved! I know it and feel it! I am LOVED! I AM love!* I became one with that love at that moment. Every cell in my body felt the love surrounding me and flowing through me and in me. I felt a sense of permanent emotional freedom from the past. I knew, without a doubt, that a power greater than me had lifted the burden of the past and taken it out of my body and out of my life. This Higher Power had removed the fear of the future off my shoulders and whisked it away as if it were light as a feather.

I turned on the light in the bathroom and squinted. It was too bright. I felt as if I were already surrounded by bright light, so I covered my tear-filled eyes and turned the overhead light off. My mind was silent. I stood there engulfed in the presence of this Love, as if bathing in the light of Love, for what seemed like a timeless moment. The joy persisted.

Slowly, my mind started back up as if someone had turned the switch back on and the gears in the machine were beginning to turn again. I realized the Truth was clear. The Truth had set me free. The power of Truth was upon me. Freedom and peace enveloped me and infused me. There was an unmistakable change in my body. I felt different. I felt … free. I felt saved. I felt filled with joy. And I knew everything was going to be okay. It was as if I were Ebenezer Scrooge when he awakened from his dream and realized he had a second chance. I was alive and well and facing a new life. I had been reborn and could start over. Reboot!

I had a new awareness about myself. I was loved and worthy of that love. How fantastic is this?

I had seen truth and felt completely changed in just ten minutes. It sounds funny now—too easy, like an infomercial promise. In just ten minutes, your life can change! But that's the power of God. My transformation was profound and nearly instantaneous compared to all the years it had taken to get me to this point.

I knew with my whole body that the emergence of my power to change was a result of my willingness to be open to new possibilities. I had opened up to what had been available all along: the power of divine, healing love, which awakened my ability to observe myself and my life differently. The burdens were gone. The Truth had set me free!

I quietly crawled back into bed and turned off the nightlight. My roommate was breathing steady and softly, and I silently lay on my back staring at the ceiling, contemplating what had just happened. I knew that the power of Truth was at the heart of the experience I'd just had. I knew that to keep this new feeling of joy and freedom alive, I would have to open up my box of secrets and let all of my demons out of their cages. I knew this was the next step in my healing process and in the recovery from my disease of addiction. Yes, I thought to myself in the darkness of my room, I've got to share my biggest secrets with the minister that will be coming tomorrow. I then quietly drifted off into a calm, serene sleep.

Several hours later, I woke up feeling fresh, and my first thought was, *Have I lost it? Is that incredible feeling of love, peace, and pure joy gone?* As I lay there on my back, I quickly started to scan my body for feelings. I felt loose and unencumbered, with the same sense of the presence of love all throughout my body. I noticed that this change made me aware of the heavy burden I had been carrying. It was only now that it was absent that I realized how great it had been. Now, my heart was warm and happy. I recognized that my newfound sense of freedom and joy had come from an unfamiliar source and reawakened my body, which had been numb for years. Despite all that had preceded this moment, despite not knowing what lay ahead, I knew I was going to be okay. I knew that transparency and honesty would be my path as I moved forward.

I had a strong urge to read the bible that I had on my nightstand. I randomly opened the bible to a page in the New Testament. The morning, spring light was now pouring into the room from the windows. I saw that I had opened the bible to the Lord's Prayer. How's that for an appropriate passage to read? I'm certain God was nudging me. *This one, Steve. Check it out!*

With a new clarity of thought and perception, I was able to understand the spiritual message written between the lines as I read the familiar prayer. *Our Father, who art in heaven.* I understood for the first time that heaven is everywhere, so God is everywhere. I create heaven here on earth and God is with me here. *Hallowed be thy name. Thy kingdom come.* The kingdom isn't out there but here—within me. And the kingdom is God's presence. *Thy will be done.* God's presence is within me so everything that is God's will is my will, and I can connect with that easily if I don't let my ego get in the way. I don't have to think or analyze situations. By connecting to "thy will," I can just know what to do: whatever is in alignment with God's will. *On earth as it is in heaven.* Heaven is in my heart, and earth is the physical plane. *Give us this day our daily bread.* We receive everything we need, not just physical sustenance, from God. God is the Source. *And forgive us our trespasses as we forgive those who trespass against us.* Love is not judgmental, so forgiveness is easy. God doesn't judge. How can God, who is all-loving, judge? It was me that was the judge, harshly judging myself. God was forgiveness. If I could love myself and others unconditionally, as God loved me, and let go of judgment, forgiveness would be natural. *And lead us not into temptation but deliver us from evil.* The evil that exists in the world is within us. Deliverance comes when we connect to God, and we do that by going within. That's where we make the connection: inside of us. And when we do, we are freed from evil. *For thine is the kingdom and the power and the glory for ever and ever.* God is all-knowing, all-powerful—and omnipresent. This was suddenly clear. The words of the Lord's Prayer were no longer simply comforting words. Amen to that!

What a blessing this all was for me! By the grace of God, I had been changed. And then the next two questions in my head were number one, was this going to be a permanent change and number two, what on earth had just happened to me? I was aware of people saying they had been reborn, as Jesus promised, but the freshness and freedom I was experiencing didn't feel religious so much as spiritual. This distinction was very clear in my mind. And I didn't feel Jesus was there, ushering me into a new life as a Christian—anyway, I was already a Christian. I had been taught that you can't experience God directly, only through Jesus, but I somehow knew that this intense, massive love that was flooding my heart and soul was God, which is the divine force of love. Maybe the minister would have some insight into whether this was a "born again" experience, and help me figure out just what it was, or how to describe it. Anyway, I was joyful and happy and ready for whatever the world had to serve up to me.

The service was held in the common room, a beautiful space with floor-to-ceiling windows through which the light streamed, Queen Anne chairs that, for a service like this one, stood alongside rows of wooden chairs so as to fit everyone. On either side of the room was a fireplace, above which was hung a huge oil painting—on one side, a painting of Bill W., and on the other facing it, a painting of Dr. Bob, the founders of AA. My heart swelled as we sang "Amazing Grace," not just because it was a beautiful song but because the words, written by a man who had come to experience God's grace, resonated for me. The minister's words and the service itself were moving, but I was eager to have a minute alone with him.

Once we had some privacy, I did my best to explain what had transpired the night before, and the minister listened without adding much, saying, "I see, uh huh," and encouraging me with his body language to keep going. As for my big question about whether this was a Christian "born again" experience or not, he was noncommittal. I guess maybe he felt it was up to me to figure it out and define it in my own way.

Then, I confessed some secrets to him that were so personal I'll never share them with anyone else. I needed to express myself, and a while back, I'd attended a lecture by the minister who had said that unlike medical records, or anything we said to the rehab counselors, anything we expressed to him as a spiritual counselor would be strictly confidential. In other words, even a subpoena couldn't get him to reveal it. I was working on steps four and five of my twelve-step program: "Made a searching and fearless moral inventory of ourselves" and "admitted to God, ourselves, and to another human being the exact nature of our wrongs." The minister was the human being I chose to make the admission to.

Afterward, I walked around in awe of the unusual and clearly spiritual experience I'd just had. I felt fresh and fully alive. I had a clean slate and was starting life anew! I understood that the truth would set me free, and I knew I could move forward on a path of total disclosure of my past.

After that, I made rapid progression in my recovery—being open, honest, and willing to listen to any new ideas. My counselor wasn't quite as convinced as I was. In fact, she wrote in my chart, "He says he's had some type of a change. I still feel that he needs to stay another week." Now, some of that might have been because they knew I was willing to stay in rehab for as long as it took to become solid enough in my recovery that I wouldn't be back through those front doors again, emptying my pockets of painkillers and in need of detox. Reading what she wrote, the old Steve might have said, "She's wrong! I'll show her!" and tried to convince her to recommend I be released. The new Steve, post awakening, understood that she was being cautious and I needed to trust her, just as I needed to trust in the twelve-step program—and trust in my Higher Power.

Clean and Sober

Chapter Twenty-One

A bout a month after my awakening, I was told I could move to a nicer building on the Marworth grounds that was less dorm-like. That was the building where those of us who were paying out of pocket to extend our rehabilitation days seemed to end up as beds became available. I would have my own bathroom and enjoy more privacy.

Just after I moved into the other building, I stopped in to see the nondenominational minister again. I had a pressing question that I wanted to ask him: "Ever since that day when I had the awakening experience I told you about, it's as if I've been physically freed from a burden that was weighing me down. I realize now that it felt like I had a concrete block, six inches thick, that encased me. I woke up this morning and the casing was gone. It was incredible. Do you think that feeling will come back?"

The minister thought for a moment. "No, I don't think it will. Because I think you experienced God's divine love, and that set you free. As long as you stay connected to God, as long as you hold on to that intention, I don't think the feeling of being surrounded by concrete will return. God can never leave you. You can only leave God. So I think you'll continue to feel God's presence."

I'm happy to say he would be proven right. I had woken up each morning after that awakening experience with the thought, *Is it gone? Am I back to feeling imprisoned and burdened? Or am I free?* I'd check in with myself and my body and sure enough, God's presence was still there. After talking to the minister, I stopped having that moment of concern upon awakening each morning. But I still sometimes wake up and think, *It's here! I feel it—the presence of God.* It is an incredible blessing to wake up and actually feel that. And I realize that's the feeling I was searching for all those years. I don't have to live in fear of losing it ever again.

To wake up every day feeling not just alive and filled with optimism, but accompanied by and infused with the divine presence of God's love, made me eager to do whatever it took to work my program. One of the rules of the rehab was that if my children were going to be allowed to visit, they had to sit through a two-hour presentation on the subject of codependency, so I asked them to help me by participating. I told Dale to bring all of them for the meeting, and they were very cooperative—even toddler Gracie, who had only the vaguest idea about what was going on. The boys were asked by the rehab counselors to identify anything they could think of that scared them about my behavior, and the only thing that came to mind for them was my getting sleepy behind the wheel of the car. It had only happened a few times, but it made an impression on them. It was clear to me, from the way they acted when they did get to see me, that I was extremely lucky that my kids were not nearly as affected by my addiction as they might have been. They were just glad I was getting help and that I'd be home after summer ended.

To me, that felt healthy and normal. I remember when my mother had back surgery when I was fifteen, I was a little scared and then I thought very little about it. I was a typical kid, absorbed in my own life, not worried about how mom was doing. Apparently, my addiction was so well hidden that it didn't much affect my kids. I felt very fortunate that my family, unlike so many others, escaped relatively unharmed by my addictive behaviors.

I was really looking forward to going home and regaining my independence. I graduated to Phase Three, and on the weekend of July 14, 2006, made my first trip back to home in York, Pennsylvania. It felt good to be home with my family, but it was also very awkward, because I felt different from how I'd felt the last time I was there. I had changed a great deal. My awakening had opened me to growing and learning, to recognizing that I could experience God directly and was never alone and disconnected from Him. My sense was, *I'm going to be okay. I am loved!*

I was very positive, and reflective, too. That was not the usual Steve, which made it difficult for Dale to relate to me, although the kids seemed to be perfectly happy to have dad home again, if only for a short time. They didn't seem to notice the changes in me, but then again, our conversations were mostly about what was going on with them.

I was vigilant about participating in my meetings, including while I was back home. I was supposed to keep my eyes open for a permanent sponsor who had been in recovery for at least a year. A good sponsor acts as a sounding board, observer, and confidant, and guides you through the recovery process as you're experiencing your challenges. One of the twelve-step meetings I went to that first weekend home was focused around people celebrating their anniversaries of sobriety. A fellow named Len was celebrating his 10th anniversary of being alcohol free. The man who was sitting with him, Ken, was his sponsor, and Ken had thirteen years of sobriety. I happened to sit in the front row, opposite these two gentlemen, and couldn't help noticing how happy they seemed, laughing and having fun. I remembered them saying in one of my instructional classes in rehab, "Go with the winners," and looking at Len and Ken, I thought, *These two guys are having so much fun that they must be winners.* I struck up a conversation with Ken, and we spoke here and there throughout the meeting. Afterward, he turned to me and said, "So are you going to ask me to be your sponsor?"

"Yes!" I responded.

So, Ken became my first sponsor. I was committed to "working the program," as they say, using techniques such as attending daily twelve-step meetings to maintain my sobriety one day at a time, so I was very glad I found Ken that weekend.

I returned to rehab looking forward to wrapping it up, but as it turns out, I was to experience a setback of sorts.

It all started when some of the weekend staff became lax about collecting cell phones: We were allowed to have them when in Phase Three and away from the rehab center visiting our families for a weekend, but we were supposed to turn them in. I came back from my first weekend away and since the staff didn't ask for my phone, I didn't volunteer it. I had it all week in my room, and had it the following weekend away as well. With no roommate, it was easy to get away with using the phone. I made some calls to my wife and to my new sponsor, Ken, who didn't realize I was breaking the "house rules" at Marworth. I also checked in with my partners to ask about some patients. My reasoning was sound except for the fact that in keeping this secret and holding on to the belief that "it's okay to break the rules because Steve's an important guy", I was potentially jeopardizing my sobriety.

Now, I had developed a dental problem so I drove out to Olyphant to have a dentist do a root canal during this period when I was secretly hoarding my phone. Then, just after my second weekend away, I developed a slight infection and received a prescription for antibiotics, which would not be available at Marworth until the following day. I asked for and received permission to go to a pharmacy to pick up the antibiotic.

As I was driving to get my antibiotics, I started to feel anxious. The pharmacy was a trigger for me. I hadn't been to one since purchasing narcotics with false prescriptions, and I was feeling that I couldn't trust myself. I'd learned that if you're experiencing fear, it can lead to relapse because you reach for drugs or alcohol to ease that uncomfortable feeling, so you should call your sponsor or someone else who attends meetings if you don't have a sponsor yet and share your feelings. I pulled out my cell phone and called Ken, but he didn't answer, so I started calling every twelve-step meeting member I could. Again and again, I got people's voicemails.

Finally, I arrived at the parking lot of the pharmacy and felt more relaxed because I had done the right thing. I checked in with how I was feeling and realized my sense of trust in myself had returned. I went in, purchased the antibiotics at the pharmacy counter, got back in my car, and drove back to rehab.

Right away, there was a group counseling meeting I was supposed to attend. I meant to stow the phone in my room, with the ringer off, but "forgot"—or maybe a part of me wanted me to forget. Or maybe God arranged the whole thing. In the middle of the meeting, my cell phone, which was still in my pocket, began to ring.

Busted.

I took it out nonchalantly and turned it off, not answering the call or checking the number. No big deal, I told myself. But there was serious fallout. The head counselor, Dominick, chose to be very serious in his punishment. I think in part he wanted to make an example of me to put a stop to other people's blatant disregard for the cell phone rules—some people were breaking the rules more often than not. And I was in the health care provider group: We were especially endangered if we relapsed because we have access to prescription drugs because of our work. You can lose your ability to process drugs when you're clean for weeks on end, so if you slip up and use again, you could die.

At first, I resented how harsh Dominick was being, but not for long. I surrendered. And looking back, I feel his reaction was sound given the risk.

As it turns out, when I finally left rehab and got my cell phone back, I checked to see who had called me. It was a wrong number! Frankly, I think it was God calling me on the cell phone with the message, "You are not above the rules, and if you think you are, you could end up in big trouble, buddy. So I'm going to make sure you learn that lesson!"

The punishment for my illicit cell phone possession was that they searched my room for drug and alcohol. I felt very insulted, and annoyed when they removed from me the privileges of Phase Three and put me back in Phase One, where I wasn't even allowed to leave the rehab facility.

I'd been told to listen to whatever my counselors said and trust their judgment, so I submitted to the punishment without protest. My wife was irritated, in part because we'd had an appointment with a psychologist the upcoming weekend and now I was restricted from leaving the grounds. That didn't sit well with Dale, but those were the rules and like everyone else, I had to follow them. There is no gray zone for an alcoholic or drug addict—especially early in recovery when the risk of relapse is very high. I was recommitted to following Good Orderly Direction—God!—and the rules. To relapse is to die—not necessarily right away, but that is where the road leads, so you have to work the program. Getting knocked back into Phase One was a lot better than the real-life punishments I would have faced had I relapsed: jail or death.

I continued to go to meetings held in a large ground floor room of the rehab center, with huge windows offering a view of the garden, so I had exposure to other members of my twelve-step program for alcoholics. I could go to twelve-step meetings for people addicted to narcotics, but I didn't feel I would ever take drugs again. The twelve-step program for alcoholics was working for me, and my counselors agreed that I was making a good choice for myself in sticking solely with that one. It's not the drug you're taking that matters so much as the reasons you're taking it—and your willingness to work a twelve-step program.

On August 9, 2006, 77 days after beginning rehab, I was discharged. I was still in Phase One because of my punishment—in fact, I was probably the only patient they ever discharged from Phase One! But my counselors and I felt I was ready. I was clean and sober, and optimistic about my new life.

I packed up my bags, filled up my SUV, and started back to York, Pennsylvania. Before I even arrived home, I went to an appointment I'd made to meet with the Physician's Health Program (PHP) at the Pennsylvania Medical Society office in Harrisburg. I'd heard that the program would help me stay sober and give me advice on fulfilling the requirements of the medical board to ensure that I wasn't using drugs or alcohol. I signed up, making a five-year commitment to be in contact with them monthly, attend meetings and keep records of my meeting attendance, and participate in a urine drug-monitoring program, where random urines could be selected on any given day. They explained that if I went on vacation, I would have to drive to the nearest designated urine collection location, or do a urine test before departing and upon returning. All that was agreeable to me.

Then, I drove over to the other side of Harrisburg and met with Josh Lock, my criminal attorney, as well as the lawyer who would be able to take advise me and represent me in dealing with medical licensing issues. First, Josh suggested we place a call to the Drug Enforcement Administration office, which was under the auspices of Pennsylvania State Attorney General Tom Corbett. That's when I was reminded of the strong possibility that Corbett, who would be running for governor, would put out a press release exposing the charges against me.

When it came to my secret going public, it wasn't me I was worried about. As I say, I was glad the truth would be out. I was tired of living a lie. I was concerned about how the news becoming public would affect my family. Would the kids be teased at school? Would my parents be embarrassed? I knew Dale would be. Would our friends stand by us? I knew that the press release might get on the Internet. At least my parents lived enough away from York that they and their friends probably wouldn't see anything on their local news broadcasts. Being in their 80s, they weren't surfing the net in their free time, so I knew it was unlikely that they'd read the press release. But maybe someone they knew would? There was nothing I could do about that.

The DEA agent was in the building, so he stopped in to meet with us. I wasn't nervous because I felt I was in good hands with Josh. The agent was very polite and cordial, and let me know that he had records of ten illegal prescriptions but was only going to charge me with one felony—interception with drug/alcohol prescriptions. That was based on the pharmacist asking me if I was Dale Heird and me lying and saying yes. Suspicious, that pharmacist had called the DEA, which started the investigation that led to my legal troubles.

I leaned over and whispered to Josh, "You know, there are more than ten prescriptions." He nodded and leaned over to tell the agent.

"I know," said the agent. "But we have enough on him."

I breathed a sigh of relief. He needed to charge me with something, but he didn't need to bury me in charges.

After we all agreed to a date when I could appear before a magistrate in the district where the felony charges would be filed, the DEA agent left and Josh said to me, "You're lucky. They could've charged you with more counts." As it was, I faced up to ten years in prison and suspension of my medical license for ten years.

I spoke for a bit with the lawyer handling medical licensing issues to let him know about my signing up with the Physicians Health Program. Then, I drove home.

I had a lot to do before going back to work in early September—a date for return my partners and I agreed upon. I was glad to have built in a small cushion of time to adjust to life back home. I was feeling fairly confident that the transition back to work would go smoothly. Meanwhile, one of my partners decided that the contracts for our vascular surgery practice weren't very well put together, and it was between me and my previous partner, who was a friend. The old contract had loose ends, so after talking to the other partner, they hired a lawyer to create a new partnership agreement. We had expanded greatly, and the newest partner wasn't even listed on our partnership papers. I was a little surprised—but their explanation of why they had done it made sense.

Dale and I had a very awkward meeting with my partners before I was scheduled to return to work. They were curt with us, and I couldn't see how the three of us were going to reach consensus as a group, which is what the contract called for. It sounded like "consensus" meant they'd make decisions, and I'd go along with them.

I hadn't really talked to them about what happened to me, and Dale was feeling protective and may have been more assertive than they expected. The next day, they told me over the phone that they weren't happy, and by the way, they were instituting a new rule: in the future, no wives were to attend meetings between the partners.

Dale was upset. She wasn't a stranger to my partners—in fact, when we didn't have an office manager for a while, she helped out. They knew her. But apparently, she rubbed them the wrong way. Their trust in me was eroded, too, which became clear when they refused to grant me the one thing I was asking for: backup for being on call in case I wasn't available. If they weren't going to agree with that … I was not okay with their decision, so I called a lawyer and, well, things deteriorated from there. The standoff lasted about a month, and I considered suing them, but then I realized I needed to move on. We were covering two hospitals, forty miles apart from each other, providing emergency and urgent surgery to their patients whenever it was needed. I wanted to reduce the amount of time I was on call, and to know someone had my back. That would reduce the stress on me that might trigger a relapse, but neither partner seemed to value what mattered most to me. Their unwillingness to compromise was a deal breaker, as far as I was concerned. So now, I was unemployed and would have to start my own practice or get a job even as my medical license was in jeopardy.

My legal problems continued. On September 29, 2006, Josh, the DEA agent, and I stood in front of the local magistrate in Shrewsbury, Pennsylvania, the town where I had committed the felony of filling a fraudulent prescription for Dale and claiming it was for me. The magistrate said he didn't consider me a flight risk so while he was setting my bail at $5000, he was suspending payment. That meant I wouldn't have to pay anything and could simply go to the courthouse in York, where I lived, and be booked.

Next, I had to drive to the sheriff's department in York and get fingerprinted and have mug shots taken. As soon as I walked in the door, I felt the weight of how serious my situation was. *I'm a criminal,* I thought. *I'm actually facing felony charges.* I'd known that intellectually, of course, but I really didn't feel it until I was there, about to undergo the same procedure that anyone who had burglarized a house or robbed someone at gunpoint had undergone. As I sat waiting for my picture to be taken, I noticed the shackles attached to the bench, and when the officer grabbed my fingers to roll the tips over an inkpad, he was brusque. I wasn't getting any special treatment from him just because

I was a middle class physician—that was appropriate, but it was humbling and sobering to go through that experience.

On the local news that evening, there was a story covering a physician in York, Steven Heird charged with a felony of fraud and it was also in the subsequent morning newspapers. We had anticipated this, but it was difficult for my wife and children. I was already in recovery and from my point of view it was old news, but facing the public revelation was anxiety provoking. The press release came out at the same time, but despite the publicity, the boys heard nothing about it at school.

I had thought about working at York Hospital. The department chairman and head of their vascular surgery department wasn't concerned about my medical license being in jeopardy, or the felony charges hanging over me. He was supportive, saying he had great respect for my work and liked me, but he would have to see how the rest of the staff felt after the news broke. Unfortunately, it turned out that some felt it was too risky to hire me, given that I now had a noticeable blemish on my reputation. He seemed to feel bad about not being able to hire me, but I thanked him for his candor. I wasn't very surprised. I just told myself, "Well, one day at a time." That motto rang true for getting through a day without a sip of alcohol or a pill. I had to trust that my legal and career situations would work out somehow.

And I was heartened by some anonymous letters of support that arrived in the mail. One letter bore a CC to the department chairman at York Hospital and expressed support for my professional conduct. I got a few phone calls of support, too. And a former patient who heard the news even sent me a book on hope. A couple of clients canceled their appointments at the vascular center, and some of our "friends" stopped talking to us, but then, they weren't good friends in the first place. As far as I was concerned, they were no great loss.

Then I discovered that without telling me, my ex-partners had cancelled my malpractice insurance. I was shocked—they didn't just let it lapse, they cancelled it! What was that about? It seemed gratuitously ugly—but maybe they simply didn't stop to think about what it would do to me. What especially upset me is that I was one of the physicians who had started that particular group, and they clearly weren't going to cut me any slack at all. Now, I not only had to find a new job but a new malpractice insurance policy if I was going to practice again. I knew I could get a policy through the state as a physician unaffiliated with a hospital or clinic, but it would be very expensive compared to the previous policy. Just what I needed—more expenses when I was bringing in no income!

In the meantime, my attorney negotiated a plea agreement with the local York county district attorney's office. They accepted a third-degree misdemeanor charge of drug possession and accepted a request to be admitted to a one-year drug court program. At the end of that program, after an additional six months of documented success and sobriety, my charges could be expunged from my record. This was a huge relief, of course.

Because my plea was accepted, I entered the drug court program in February of 2007 for one year. I was also advised by a wonderful soccer mom I knew through my kids—a woman who was also an attorney who had worked for the state board of medical licensing—that I would benefit from enrolling in the Pennsylvania Health Monitoring Program, PHMP, even though I was in the Physicians Health Program. PHMP is a monitoring program run by the licensing board of the state of Pennsylvania to monitor drug and alcohol recovery in professional licensed people, and having a track record of being in it and compliant would help me maintain my license. I was told I'd have to stay in that program for three years. I was also going to end up being in the drug court program, which would last for a year and require me to show up in court every Thursday with the other defendants as part of my probation, and give a weekly urine sample.

I was on probation, which meant I couldn't leave the county without permission, not even to see my parents in Maryland. It also meant I couldn't have any firearms or alcohol in the house. Dale moved her wine to a neighbor's garage. As for guns, well, I didn't own any, so that wasn't a problem. Reading the rules of probation was another reminder of how I was officially a criminal, and in the eyes of the law, I wasn't to be trusted until I could prove myself trustworthy again.

I was following the rules of all the drug monitoring programs and giving urine samples whenever they were requested. In fact, there was one day I call the "trifecta" day when I had to give urine samples to fulfill the requirements of all three monitoring programs. I drank quite a lot of water that day!

I realized that setting up my own surgery practice would make it much easier for me to do scheduled urine tests as well as to do them on call. If I was in surgery, or one was scheduled, there was still time to get over to the lab to give a specimen according to their rules.

It took a lot of juggling to do the tests, show up in court every Thursday, go to the drug court meeting each week, and do my own recovery support meetings. But one of the programs would only be for a year, the other would end after three, and the last would end for me after five years clean and sober. In the meantime, I was determined to comply to all the rules. That included meeting with my parole officer every week. Fortunately, my electronic calendar could synch up with my computer, because my schedule was incredibly complex and I sure couldn't afford to forget any appointments. Once I opened my practice in June 2007, my calendar would start to fill up with patient appointments, too. But I felt ready for that.

If I was going to experience a relapse, I felt it would be with alcohol, not pills. Pills were harder to access, and the obstacles to attaining them would slow me down and helping me to notice that I'd triggered a desire to use them. But alcohol would be readily available in any corner store, and at home. Dale and I talked about that. She trusted me when I said I wouldn't find a way to drink. I'm happy to say I didn't betray that trust.

In the months after rehab, I tried talking to Dale about my awakening the transformation I'd undergone, but it was difficult for her to understand what I was saying or muster enthusiasm about the new Steve. She was carrying a lot of guilt and shame about me and my behavior. She'd hated having to make excuses for my inability to stay awake at social events, or not being able to attend them at all. The fact is that much of the challenge with my schedule hadn't been because I was drinking or abusing prescription drugs, but simply because I was in medical training and, later, a surgeon on call. To her, the issue wasn't my addiction so much as my disappointing her by not being who she wanted me to be. She didn't like that I couldn't create the kind of life she felt she should have and not having it bothered her—a lot. She couldn't understand how I had become free from shame, regret, or anger. The two of us were not having a meeting of minds or hearts. I felt as if she thought I'd interrupted her plans, or tarnished the public image of our family. What I was saying about having a direct experience of God without Jesus as an intermediary seemed to leave her bewildered. I had made a radical change in my attitude toward life and in my willingness to be honest and speak the truth, and she wasn't prepared for that, which is understandable.

Meanwhile, one of the stressors I faced constantly was financial stress. I hadn't felt financial pressure for several years. Once my new practice opened in February 2007, I felt confident that I would get out of debt by rebuilding my practice. But Dale's confidence in me was badly eroded. I'm sure my skill at hiding my drug use contributed to her difficulty in trusting me. She wanted me to go back to having a steady, predictable income, which my booming practice had provided me. She wasn't happy that I had said no to an offer from a hospital in Harrisburg, Pennsylvania, the previous fall. I just knew that being on call was going to be too much of a strain on me and might jeopardize my recovery, and I simply couldn't risk that. I had total faith that my new practice, which involved new technologies for treating varicose veins and didn't require hospital stays and emergencies, would be lucrative in no time. I had gotten malpractice insurance again, at a reasonable rate, through the old group, so I could drop the expensive state-backed policy. Every day was getting better, but I didn't realize that Dale's perceptions were very different from mine.

I was about to receive a harsh reality check.

Chapter Twenty-Two

Endings and Beginnings

A fter leaving Marworth, I was so excited about my new experience of God's presence that I was telling everyone I could. Some people were uncomfortable—my wife among them. But how could I help myself? I've become more discreet in the last few years, but given how intense and life changing it was, it's no wonder I was like a puppy wanting to go up to people with my tail wagging to tell them my story of feeling God's presence. "Thanks for sharing, Steve," they would say politely. I'm sure a few wished they had a tennis ball or stick to throw. But a few probably benefitted from my speaking my truth.

I believed that the truth would set me free, so I felt it necessary to explain my past and my use of drugs to my wife, which dismayed her. She couldn't comprehend my addictive, secretive behavior. She'd had no idea how much I'd been using prescription painkillers, right under her nose. As the months passed, I recognized that I was upsetting her more by being honest than by being silent and in a state of nondisclosure, which was a balance that I found myself having to walk. Her attitude seemed to be,

"Look, I'm dealing with the fallout of your behavior, I don't understand your twelve-step program talk, and I just want things to go back to the way they were." How could I blame her? Her life had been working for her. And now, she was constantly worried about the money and had a lot of fear and anger. She couldn't emotionally accept my logic that within a few months, everything would sort itself out financially and legally.

In February of 2007, when my practice opened, my wife was supposed to be the official manager of my practice, but it soon became clear that my vision wasn't hers. We had a disagreement and I asked her not to be a part of the practice—I could get someone to take calls and do the administrative work, and that would take pressure off of our relationship with each other.

Now, the tension between us was thick. I had started sleeping on a couch in our family room. We both knew we needed to talk about what was going on, so we had a painful conversation about our marriage. I truly believed that I was committed to marriage for life. I took my marriage vows very seriously and did not believe in divorce—at least, not for me. And I know Dale was very committed to our marriage, too.

But frankly, I felt I was getting more emotional support from my sponsor, Ken. And since Ken had great computer skills, he started to help me out with my practice. Dale wasn't particularly warm to him, although of course, she was polite. I'm sure it bothered her that he was working in my office and she wasn't welcome to work with me there.

Several months later, in the summer, I had to purchase some equipment and wrote a large check from our home equity loan account. I had run our credit cards up to the limit, feeling confident that I could get out of the red and back into the black in the fall. Dale apparently didn't share my confidence. Instead of having a conversation, she stopped payment on it. I found this out when the check bounced and I called the bank.

When I talked to her that night, Dale explained she had done it because she wasn't comfortable with the financial choices I was making. I felt she was trying to control me and that this was a sign we needed marriage counseling. It's one thing to not be on the same page as a couple. It's another when your communication breaks down to the point where you don't broach difficult topics before taking action.

"There's hope," said the marriage counselor we consulted with. "But you two are very far apart."

Dale and I talked, and I told her that I felt she needed to address her codependency just as I had addressed my addiction—not just for our family's sake, or my sake, but for her sake. She listened and decided she would do a weeklong codependency workshop in the fall. By then, I would be making money and paying bills, I said, so our finances should be on the upswing.

In fact, as summer turned to fall, my new business began to take off. The credit cards were almost paid off. Eagerly, I took a booth at a local health expo to drum up even more business. I sat there for most of a Sunday, happily conversing with the people who stopped by to learn more about what my new center had to offer. Then, one of the neighbors said, "I'm so sorry about your divorce, by the way."

My face must have registered confusion.

"I read about it in the paper this morning, under legal notices. I hope everything goes well for you," she said with a sympathetic smile.

I managed not to stutter as I thanked her for her good wishes, and kept my mind from spinning in circles while I finished out the afternoon. Later, at home, I learned that Dale had decided to serve me divorce papers again—it's just that her attorney had neglected to prepare them when someone from his office called the newspaper to publish the legal notice.

We met with the marriage counselor we'd hired—an established expert who had written a book or two and was supposed to be excellent. I sat there as she asked Dale to say what she thought was wrong with the marriage, and listened to a long tale of how terrible a husband I had been. I guess my turn to list complaints was next, but we ran out of time in the session. And as I thought about it, I had run out of steam, too. I just couldn't continue being married when Dale and I were so far apart from each other and there were so few signs that we could reconcile. And the marriage counselor did say to me, "As far as your children are concerned, two stable homes are better than one unstable home." She explained that kids pick up on the tension between their parents, so staying together under the circumstances was just causing them stress. Her words made sense. I didn't want to be a failure at marriage, but it was more important to protect my children from emotional agitation that was sure to go on and on.

I was starting to realize my fear of failure had been set in childhood—in infancy, really. I was a second child in a household under stress. It was a challenge for my mom to be a busy farm wife, care for the son she already had, and attend to me when I cried to be fed, changed, or picked up. That's certainly not a criticism of her; it's just how it was. Not being old enough to understand that she truly wanted to meet all my needs, and just wasn't able; I learned that attention, affection, and love had to be earned. I had to do something to get my basic needs met. Of course, I can look at that as an adult and know that's irrational, but it's my infant self-perceived belief—that I have to earn love—became embedded in my unconscious mind and drove much of my behavior throughout my life. It was a belief I had to consciously recognize and reject.

In September 2008, as my kids all began a new school year—Grace in Kindergarten, Billy at College, and Andrew and Jonathan in junior and senior high, Dale began a new school year as a teacher. And I began the school of living by myself—in an apartment I rented not too far from the house, which Dale put on the market. Two of my drug programs had been completed, and I was continuing to go to meetings. I was devouring book after book on spirituality and discovering authors such as Deepak Chopra and Eckhart Tolle. *The Secret,* which I found on a table at a local bookstore, taught me about the Law of Attraction. I was hungry to learn as much as possible about God and my relationship with him. I wanted to co-create a new life and reclaim my sense of purpose as someone who helps others to heal. My initial attraction to being a surgeon was to help others to overcome their ailments, but I was now broadening what that meant.

I enjoyed having a thriving surgical practice, but I was thinking about other ways in which I could serve as a healer besides just being a surgeon. My understanding of myself and my relationship to the universe was growing and expanding at an incredible rate. My sense of abundance just kept increasing, and it was mirrored in my work, my relationships, and my finances.

In January 2009, the last of my legal problems were resolved; I was free of probation. Two of the three monitoring programs had ended, and I would continue in the last one for another couple of years. I knew my name was on a national drug registry, available on the Internet, so anyone searching for information on me could learn about my past. It didn't matter, though. I was free of the dark, ugly secret of my addiction. My family had adjusted to the new reality that I was a recovering addict and alcoholic. Occasionally, a patient will call and cancel an appointment, citing that they heard what I did—and that's okay with me. If they're not comfortable with me, so be it. In the vast majority of cases, people seem fine with the fact that I went through recovery.

My anonymity had been broken but that means I have no fear of being exposed. I know I am not the same Steve who was taking painkillers and chasing them with alcohol.

Addiction is a disease, a medical condition, and therefore protected by HIPAA laws. Thousands of physicians in the U.S. are addicted to drugs or alcohol but their patients don't know it. These doctors are probably terrified of being exposed, but I don't have to feel that way anymore. I'm free.

But I'm always aware that addiction can creep back and swallow me up again. I'm aware of my triggers, and I maintain my sobriety one day at a time. I read spiritual books and meditate. I'm awake and living mindfully.

My divorce was finalized on December 31, 2010. I've let go of my disappointment in not being able to make it work. At one point, my wife told me, "I liked you better when you were drinking and using drugs." That was incredibly painful to hear, but I knew what she was saying. She had been content with her life as it was, even if it wasn't working for me. It was going to come crashing down at some point as my addiction progressed. I know that if I get married again, I will marry someone who loves me for who I am today, who doesn't think of me as a worthless drug addict or a disappointment simply because I sometimes let down the people I love. I am not my actions. I don't identify with what I did in the past. And we all make mistakes and have weaknesses. At least I can say that every day, I wake up happy to be given another chance at life, another chance to do better, grow more, and serve my community.

Every day offers me another chance to be the best father I can be. Every day presents an opportunity for me to smell the incredible scent of freshly mown grass, to experience what it's like to zoom down a snowcapped mountain on my skis, or to feel the sun against my skin as I'm reminded of what a marvelous creation I am a part of. And every day, I wake up and feel that the sense of being encased and trapped is long gone. Spirit is next to me, around me, inside me, making my lungs fill with air, making my heart beat, and pushing the blood through my veins.

What more could I ask for?

Twelve Prescriptions
for Awareness

When it comes to wellness at every level—body, mind, and spirit—awareness is absolutely crucial. It is the key that will unlock your prison and set you free. It's what will set you on the course to living with greater joy, abundance, and purpose.

As a physician, I believe that whatever you think your problem is, however you define it, awareness is the number one prescription. If you're not aware of what you're doing and what your power is, how are you going to resolve your problem?

When I finally faced my addiction, I woke up to some challenging truths about myself and my problems. It was hard to face many of those truths, but I'm glad I did.

So what do you need to become aware of? Well, to start you off, let me give you twelve prescriptions for awareness that I think will go a long way toward helping you to live a better life. Whatever your diagnosis, these twelve prescriptions for awareness will awaken you to a new, healthier, more fulfilling way of living.

Prescription for Awareness #1:
Be aware that the truth will set you free.

I felt imprisoned by my life until the truth about my addiction was out in the open. As scared as I was when I realized the Drug Enforcement Administration was on to me and my secret had been revealed, I was relieved, too. I didn't even realize that I had come to feel encased like a mummy in heavy energy that surrounded my body. My awakening experience that night at Marworth Treatment Center made me aware of that feeling when it ended suddenly. I didn't know how trapped I had felt until my "prison" suddenly disappeared! I was liberated when God revealed to me an all-important truth: that I am a spiritual being having a temporary human experience, and I'm always connected to God. Knowing that frees me from the suffering that I created for myself—and I created a lot of suffering for myself!

Becoming aware of the power of truth opens you to possibilities for your life that you just can't see when you're living a lie, detached from God and the truth about who you are and what your choices are doing to you. Open yourself up to your Higher Power and the truth about who you are and your connection to that Higher Power. You may not have a sudden moment of awareness as I did that night when I had my awakening—yours may be more gradual—but you will feel your heart opening to the truth and the chains that are binding you beginning to break.

Prescription for Awareness #2:
Be aware of the hell you are creating for yourself.

We create hell for ourselves when we buy into the belief that we are disconnected from a Higher Power. Hell is a state of unawareness.

The pain of feeling disconnected from God, and living without awareness of the truth of my spiritual nature, was unbearable for me. In fact, it was hell on earth. When I couldn't get out of my car that day to cross the lawn to sit in the stands and cheer on my son as he played baseball, I was in hell—and it was a hell of my own creation. My stinking thinking and my disease had created it. The painkillers and alcohol created a depressive brain chemistry that mirrored my depressive feelings and thoughts. My body, my mind, and my heart were all in a state of depression.

Reconnecting to Spirit was the key to getting me out of my hellish prison and keeping me out of it.

Now, I wasn't *consciously* creating hell for myself. But I choose to hold myself responsible for all the choices I was making—including the choice to put those painkillers in my mouth when my inner voice was screaming at me, "Don't do it!" By holding myself responsible for creating my hell, I acknowledge the importance of being aware of all the choices I make. That keeps me committed to being aware of how I can easily slip back to my old habit of creating hell for myself.

When have you created hell for yourself? Are you creating hell for yourself today by denying an important truth about yourself? What is that truth?

Own your truth. It's your get-out-of-hell-free card!

Prescription for Awareness #3: Be aware that there's a karmic price to pay for trying to avoid pain at all times.

When I was drinking and using drugs, I was searching for that perfect state of euphoria so I wouldn't have to feel discomfort or pain. No matter how often I got high, it wasn't going to be enough for me. That's the addiction—despite the price you pay for getting high, you want to deny that cost and just keep getting high. When you can't get high any more and you just need the drugs and alcohol to function, you are starting to pay the price of your addiction through side effects and making bad choices by chasing after the elusive high.

The choice to keep seeking happiness and freedom from pain creates a vacuum. Eventually, that vacuum has to get filled—and all your happiness gets sucked into it. The bigger the vacuum, the bigger the karmic blowback. The more you avoid suffering, the worse the suffering will be when you finally experience it. I created quite a bubble of avoidance. When it burst, I had to deal with legal issues, the potential loss of my career—and the ultimate loss of my marriage and my business. Paying your karmic debt isn't fun—or avoidable.

Now, I know that suffering is a necessary part of life. We can't avoid it, but we can face it and learn from it. Then we'll be able to return to happiness.

In America, we've developed a culture that encourages us to avoid pain at all costs. The "pursuit of happiness" is written into the Declaration of Independence, but happiness isn't something we should *pursue*. It's something we *choose*. And even if we choose it, there are going to be times when we suffer. Happiness isn't an end goal or something permanent. Try to deny that, and avoid all pain, and happiness will elude you.

As a teenager, I had a poster in my bedroom of a butterfly in a garden, and the poster said, "Happiness is like a butterfly. The more you pursue it, the more it eludes you. When you sit quietly, it will lightly land on your shoulder." Maybe I should have spent more time staring at that poster!

What is happiness to you? Do you have to feel fantastic every minute of the day to be happy?

Prescription for Awareness #4:
Be aware that you can't make others happy.

I thought I was responsible for making others happy, but none of us can make other people happy. When we try to achieve this impossible goal, we get overwhelmed by life. Being a people pleaser will burn you out.

I didn't want to make my wife unhappy by showing up at the last minute for my son's graduation, but maybe if I had shown up my son would've been happier. I definitely would've been happier. But I was so busy trying to please everyone else I didn't take into account what would have pleased *me*.

Trying to determine the action that will make everyone happy will drive you crazy because you simply can't make everyone happy. In fact, you can't make any one person happy! You can only do your best to set the stage for others to be happy while taking care of your own needs, too. After that, happiness is every individual's responsibility. Don't take on the burden of making others happy.

When the people I cared about—my family, friends, patients, and partners—felt bad, I felt bad, and then I tried harder to make them happy. I was assigning myself an impossible task. When I learned to let go of the need to please everybody all the time, I found I was a lot happier.

Did you ever try to make everyone around you happy? Did you succeed? What did you learn from that experience?

Prescription for Awareness #5:
Be aware that you can't control other people.

We've all heard that old saying, "You can lead a horse to water, but you can't make him drink." But we sure try to force that horse to drink! At my first twelve-step meeting when I was in rehab, one of the speakers said, "Alcoholism is the only diagnosis that has to be made by the person with the disease to experience successful treatment." If someone you care about isn't ready to admit "I'm an alcoholic," you can't force them to admit it—or get treatment. All you can do is lead that horse to water.

If my wife and parents had known I had a problem with drugs and alcohol, they could have chosen to confront me. They could have done an intervention, which is a formal way of confronting an addict with love and firmness to try to get him to agree to go into rehab. But even if they had done an intervention, there's no guarantee I would have admitted to my problem or gone for help. People who are forced into rehab are more likely to relapse than people who enter voluntarily.

If you know someone whose drug and alcohol use are causing problems for that person and you consider doing an intervention—realize that if you do one, you're only leading a horse to water. If you can accept that, you will be much less hurt and frustrated if the person refuses to get help—or gets help but then relapses. You can't control other people, but you can try to awaken them to the truth about themselves.

Have you ever tried to control someone else and get that person to see things as you see them? How did that work out? Are you glad you spoke up? If you could go back, would you address the problem differently? How would you address it so that you were just leading a horse to water instead of trying to make him drink?

Prescription for Awareness #6:
Be aware that you cocreate your reality.
The universe responds to what you think about and create in your mind, whether you create that thought or idea consciously or unconsciously. If you want to change your external reality, you have to change your internal reality—and that includes changing what you're unconsciously creating. This is because of the Law of Attraction, a universal principle that works whether you realize it or not.

When I was doggedly determined to get into medical school somehow, my belief that I belonged in medical school got sent out to the universe, which responded by putting opportunities in my path. Someone who had exactly the information I needed to get to the next step in my journey to getting into medical school would show up—sitting down next to me in a college office or at a sports game. Back then, I thought these were lucky breaks. Now, I know that I was cocreating those opportunities with the help of Spirit. Then again, Spirit and I also cocreated a lot of drama together. I attracted more than one car accident, more than one situation where I got a fist in my face or a kick in my butt that didn't feel very good.

Considering how strong the Law of Attraction is, it's really important to be aware of the messages you're sending that are cocreating your reality. You want to create a reality where positive opportunities come your way, not a reality full of opportunities to get hurt and experience loss. Suffering will lead you to growth if you experience it mindfully and open yourself to its lessons. If you live mindfully and courageously, you can learn your lessons without having all the drama and trauma that makes you miserable. Pay attention to your thoughts, both the conscious ones and unconscious ones.

Do you have a conscious intention that you would like to see manifested? Do you truly believe you can achieve that goal? Or is there a part of you that doesn't believe it's possible? If you don't believe it, you can't achieve it.

Prescription for Awareness #7: Be aware that Spirit will bring you what you need in order to grow.

Spirit co-creates your reality and may answer your prayers and intentions in ways that bring you great joy. I said to myself that night before my awakening, "God, I want what that fellow has. He's walking out of rehab tomorrow a changed man." God answered that prayer by awakening me to my relationship with my spiritual self and with God. But Spirit also has much more wisdom and perspective than you do and will present you with situations that cause you enough fear and suffering to push you to make the changes you need to make. I'd had many wake-up calls about my drinking and addictive behavior, from car accidents to losing a tooth when I angrily accosted a stranger when I was drunk. God loved me enough to keep nudging me, harder and harder, until the day when the DEA showed up at my office and I finally accepted that I had to face my addiction. Apparently, I needed more than one wake-up call. Eventually, God had to throw the alarm clock at my thick head to wake me up.

Is there something in your life that was painful and scary but woke you up to your need to grow? Did you have wake-up calls before that day that you had dismissed? What was it about that last wake-up call that made you face what you had to face once and for all?

Prescription for Awareness #8: Be aware that if you open up to and experience Spirit's love, you will truly recognize that you are deserving of love and you are loved unconditionally.

I know now that I was always trying to win love from other people. It wasn't until God blessed me with His grace, making me feel His unconditional love for me, that I truly realized I was lovable just as I am with all my flaws—and that this is true of everyone. Spirit opened my eyes to the fact that every single one of us is deeply loved—and deeply lovable.

If you don't love yourself, you can end up doing terrible things to yourself and others. You can get into a vicious circle of doing something awful, feeling guilty and ashamed and unlovable, going into denial in order to avoid the pain of self-loathing, and then unconsciously doing something awful again. Being in denial and pain is no way to live—but many of us live that way because we don't recognize that we are worthy of love.

When you know you're worthy of love, you find you can love and forgive yourself. That's when the vicious circle breaks apart, the denial falls away, and you have a real shot at changing your behavior.

Do you feel worthy of love? Do you love yourself unconditionally? Can you imagine opening yourself to Spirit and asking God to help you to feel loved? Can you commit to opening your heart to Spirit so that Spirit can rush in and make you actually feel how deeply loved you are?

Prescription for Awareness #9:
Be aware that whatever you need, you will find it within.
Spirit can give you whatever you need, but you have to be willing to be still and look within to find it—because it's inside us that we experience our connection to God, the Source of all we will ever need. When you do look within, you open the door for Spirit to fill your heart. Your connection to Spirit is never broken. You can fool yourself into believing it's not there, but it is.

I thought that since I didn't feel a connection to God, God—if He existed, which I wasn't totally sure of at that point—must have abandoned me. Or maybe he was just busy with people who had bigger problems than I had. Being raised with religious beliefs didn't prevent me from growing up to feel disconnected from God. My problem was that I thought the disconnection was real, and the only thing to do was to find something outside of me to fill the hole in my heart that only Spirit could fill.

I was always chasing after something that I couldn't put my finger on. I had success, but didn't feel successful. I wanted to be happy, but happiness always seemed to escape my grasp unless I had my fingers around a bottle or had a couple of painkillers in my hand. Drugs and alcohol gave me a temporary illusion of happiness. They allowed me to stop and be in the moment, but in that stillness, I didn't go within. The sense of restlessness would return quickly. Then I would run around looking for something to make me feel better. I had to experience the stillness of having my life grind to a halt before I was ready to look within and begin talking to God again. Don't make my mistake.

Do you have a relationship with a Higher Power? When was the last time you tried to reconnect? Could you slow down, stop, and open yourself to experiencing your connection today?

Prescription for Awareness #10: Be aware of what stinking thinking is and that the way out of it is to let go of denial and surrender to the truth.

Stinking thinking is the result of the disease of addiction, whether it's addiction to a substance, a behavior, or a way of operating. If you're addicted to alcohol or people pleasing or lying, you will find yourself in stinking thinking. Stinking thinking is the idea that you are in control of your behavior, and if you just think a little more and get really clever, you'll be just fine. Stinking thinking is denial.

I was in stinking thinking when I told myself it was only dark liquor I had to avoid, or that I could drink while on call "just this once," or that I could break the rehab rules without risking relapse. In addiction, the ego has run amuck and is making a fool of itself. Inevitably, everything you deny just pops up again as if you were playing a game of Whac-a-Mole.

To get out of stinking thinking, or denial, you have to surrender to Spirit who will remind you that you are loved, restore your faith that you can trust in Spirit, and show you the next step on your journey out of hell and into sanity and freedom from addiction and suffering. The first step of the twelve steps is to admit you're powerless over your addiction. Stinking thinking makes you say, "I can control it." The paradox is that once you admit your powerlessness, you regain your real power—to work with Spirit to get your life back on track.

Do you have an addiction? Are you in control? Are you thinking you can overcome it by yourself? Are you ready to admit you could use some help from Spirit, who can do anything?

Prescription for Awareness #11:
Be aware that you are already forgiven.

I was raised a Christian and taught to forgive others, but I never realized how important it is to forgive yourself. When I got clean and sober, I was fortunate to have an awakening experience in which I accepted that I didn't have to forgive myself because I was already forgiven. God had forgiven me. And I hadn't even had a chance yet to ask him to forgive me!

It's important to know that you're forgiven because it allows you to break out of denial and face the things you've done that you feel guilty about. Feeling forgiven and loved gives you the courage to start making amends to other people, which is part of any twelve-step program. Making amends is something we all have to do. And just when we think we've crossed off our list the name of everyone we owe an apology and amends to, we'll manage to screw up and do something that will require a new round of saying, "I'm sorry" and offering to make amends. When you realize how easy it is to screw up, it can be hard not to get discouraged.

In a TED talk, Brené Brown, a researcher on guilt and shame, says the following about the difference between the two: guilt is the feeling you get when you think, "I made a mistake" and shame is the feeling you get when you think, "I am a mistake." You are not your mistakes. You are a spiritual being having a temporary human experience, and while you're here, you are going to make mistakes. The moment you make a mistake, God forgives you. Your job is to recognize your mistake as soon as you can and forgive yourself so that you can do what you need to do to make up for it. Getting stuck in guilt or shame serves no one. In fact, it just leads to more mistakes, guilt, and shame.

Is there something you haven't forgiven yourself for? If there is, say this prayer: "Thank you, Spirit (or God, or Higher Power), for loving me enough to have forgiven me already. Help me to forgive myself."

Prescription for Awareness #12: Be aware that you can find your purpose and new ways to express it if you're willing to open your heart to Spirit.

As a child, I was fortunate to discover my purpose early on. I knew I was called to become a doctor and to help people who were sick or hurting. But like most people, I interpreted my purpose too literally, and got stuck in trying to be a certain type of surgeon rather than a doctor who helps lead people back to wellness. And I forgot that at the heart of being a doctor is being a healer. The Latin root of the word "doctor" means to lead, not to fix or cure. A doctor leads you in your self-healing. You have to do your part. The doctor can't be responsible for every choice you make about your health.

Because I was too literal about my purpose, I couldn't see a way out of the life I created for myself. A surgeon is expected to be on call to perform life-or-death surgeries, but you can be a surgeon without having to be in a constant state of concern that you may have to drop everything and rush off to save someone's life. You can be a doctor without being a surgeon. And you can be a healer without being a doctor. I have a huge range of possibilities open to me that will allow me to live according to my purpose, but I couldn't see that before.

To take care of myself as well as others, I had to change the kind of healer I am. I'm discovering new ways to help people who are sick or hurting—and I'm doing it without driving myself so hard that I feel depleted and empty.

Do you know what your purpose is? Can you open up to Spirit revealing your purpose? And are you willing to be creative in expressing your purpose, whatever it is?

• • •

The truth that set me free was the awareness of who I was, of my power to create a prison for myself or liberate myself with the help of Spirit. The truth was that I'm never alone, never unloved, and never in need of looking outside myself for happiness.

My relationship to Spirit is at the center of my life now. So is my relationship with me. You see, my relationship with Spirit and my relationship with myself are the same thing, because I'm part of Spirit. We all are. If I don't take care of myself—if I don't follow that saying "Physician, heal thyself"—I can't heal others. I can't live according to my purpose if I'm not taking care of Steve.

And I want to live according to my purpose. My healing work isn't done. It's just taking a different form. I'm still going to help the sick and troubled. I'm still going to use my skills and knowledge to help people experience the free flow of the loving life force that is Spirit. I want to help people clear the blocks to experiencing that flow of divine love that eradicates depression and suffering and that opens us to living fully and joyfully. And thanks to Spirit being there for me, nourishing my own creativity, I know there are endless ways I can do that. For the opportunity to heal myself and others, I am deeply grateful. I found my happiness, and it's in living my purpose. I hope that I have in some small way given you insight into how to find and live your purpose—and reconnect with Spirit.

If you feel moved to become a part of my circle of healing and share your wisdom and support as you participate in fellowship, please contact me at **www.prescriptionsforawareness.com** *or on* **www.facebook.com/steven. heird**. *I hope you'll join me in the work of healing!*

About the Author

Steven B. Heird, M.D., F.A.C.S. holds certifications in general surgery and the specialty of vascular surgery. He has devoted his skills and expertise to his private practice while expanding his spiritual and holistic approaches to life and medicine. After a stay in a rehabilitation hospital to overcome the power of addiction, Steve is enlightened to share his message of hope and recovery through a spiritual light which emanates from his passion for public speaking, group discussions, and interviews for local publications.

Steve grew up in Hampstead, Maryland and attended the University of Maryland School of Medicine in Baltimore, Maryland. He then resided in York, Pennsylvania where he completed his surgical residency. Following his residency, he lived in Philadelphia, Pennsylvania while participating in a fellowship in vascular surgery at the Hospital of the University of Pennsylvania. He has now returned to York, Pennsylvania where he has owned and operated his vascular specialty practice for many years.

CPSIA information can be obtained at www.ICGtesting.com
Printed in the USA
BVOW03s1424010315

389815BV00004B/178/P

9 781630 472344